How Meera Built an Accounting Practice that Gave Her More Money, Financial and Time Freedom

PRACTICE!

Noel Guilford, BA FCA

Practice!

How Meera built an accounting practice that gave her more money, financial and time freedom

Copyright ©2025 Noel Guilford

First published March 2025 by Guilford Accounting Limited, Chester, England, CH4 9LF

https://guilfordaccounting.co.uk

Paperback ISBN: 978-0-9933678-4-7

Kindle ISBN: 978-0-9933678-5-4

Cover Design and Interior Formatting by 100 Covers

All rights reserved. No part of this publication may be reproduced, stored in, or introduced into a retrieval system, or transmitted in any form or by any means, electronic or mechanical, including photocopying, recording or otherwise without prior written permission of the publishers.

The web addresses referenced in this publication were live and correct at the time of the book's publication but may be subject to change.

GET YOUR FREE PRACTICE HEALTH CHECKLIST

Complete my practice health assessment checklist

Assess the health of your practice – or find out what best practice looks like for a digital accountancy practice – by completing my practice health assessment checklist. Find your gaps and prepare a practice improvement action plan: https://bit.ly/practice-health-check.

Contents

Introduction vii
A Meeting That Changed Everything 1
The Seven Principles 9
Regulatory and Compliance Essentials 15
Meera maps out her Business Model 21
Quality Over Quantity 29
Getting Clients 35
The Discovery Call 47
Google Business Profile 53
Onboarding a New Client 59
Getting the Right Tech Stack 65
AI and the Power of Prompting and Automation 71
Setting up her Home Office 79
The First 90 Days 85
Resources 91
Acknowledgements 147
About the Author 151

INTRODUCTION

I began my career in accountancy at a small two-partner firm in Barrow in Furness, working while studying for my accountancy degree. It was a traditional practice—the kind where ledgers were still handwritten, client records filled filing cabinets, and tax returns were manually compiled. Despite the passage of time and industry-wide digital transformation, many accountancy firms today still resemble that early practice.

After qualifying as a Chartered Accountant with Arthur Andersen & Co., I opened an office for Spicer & Pegler (now part of Deloitte) in Chester. Over the next decade, I became a partner at one of the world's largest accountancy firms deciding in 2002 to start my own practice, Guilford Accounting. That decision changed everything.

Over the years, I've seen first-hand how the profession has evolved—and, more importantly, how many accountants and bookkeepers have been slow to embrace the digital revolution. Yet, those who *have* harnessed modern technology and automation have transformed their businesses, dramatically improving efficiency, client service, and profitability.

Today, a sole practitioner working virtually or for a small firm with a remote team can compete head-on with larger firms. By developing robust digital systems and processes, they can streamline workflows, attract high-value clients, and build a profitable, sustainable practice—without sacrificing their personal life.

That's what this book is about.

Rather than presenting you with another technical guide full of theory and abstract principles, I've chosen to teach through storytelling. This book follows the journey of Meera, a skilled accountant embarking on the challenge of building her own digital-first practice, with guidance from her experienced mentor, David.

This format allows readers to learn more effectively by losing themselves in a story and by being able to relate to the characters. It also helps them understand how the principles can be applied in a non-theoretical real-world environment. Through Meera's experiences—the successes, the setbacks, and the lessons learned—you'll see how to apply these same strategies to your own practice.

At the end of each chapter, you'll find a summary of the key points and actionable steps. While it may be tempting to skip them or quickly skim through, these exercises are designed to accelerate your progress. Completing them will make the following chapters more impactful.

But the actions are there to help you progress faster, not to slow you down! They're like building blocks and will make the future chapters and actions in the book easier to complete because of the momentum you'll build as you go. If you take time to give each action careful consideration and write down your answers so you can refer to them later, the better this book will work for you.

Following the story, you'll find Resources packed with practical insights to help you implement the concepts covered in the book and details about how you can work with me.

Whether you're considering starting your own practice or looking to transform an existing practice, the guidance here is drawn directly from my experience - not only as a big-4 partner - but also from building two successful firms from the ground up.

I hope you enjoy following Meera and David's journey—and that, by the end of this book, you'll feel inspired and equipped to create an accountancy practice that gives you more money, financial and time freedom.

To your success.

Noel Guilford
March 2025

A Meeting That
Changed Everything

It had been an emotional few weeks for Meera. Leaving behind the security of a well-respected regional accountancy practice to strike out on her own felt like the biggest decision of her life. Now, having worked her notice, said her goodbyes to her clients, and shared farewell drinks with colleagues who had become friends, she stood at the edge of a new chapter—both nervous and excited about what lay ahead.

She had no doubt about her technical ability. As a Chartered Accountant with years of experience across diverse clients and assignments, she knew she could deliver quality work. But running a business? That was a new challenge entirely.

In the evenings and at weekends, she had thrown herself into research, absorbing as much as she could about setting up an accountancy practice. The more she read, the more overwhelmed she became. There was so much to consider—marketing, pricing, technology, and client onboarding. She had always assumed that being a great accountant would be enough. Now, she was realising that it was just one piece of a much bigger puzzle.

One particularly insightful paper she'd found online, *What's More Important Than Your Life*, had helped her step back from the mechanics of running a practice and focus on the bigger picture. It guided her to document *why* she wanted to start her own firm, define her vision, and identify the types of clients she wanted to serve. That clarity strengthened her resolve—but it hadn't erased her doubts.

During her research, she had also come across an event hosted by her local Accountants Society. She had been a member for years but had never attended one of their events, as her firm had always provided its own training. But this one—*The Digital Firm of the Future*—had caught her eye. On a whim, she had booked a ticket. Now the day had arrived, and she was debating whether she had the nerve to actually go.

If she was serious about starting her own practice, she reasoned, she would have to get used to networking events and introducing herself to strangers. This was as good a time as any to start.

At the hotel where the event was being held, she took a deep breath and pushed open the door to the meeting room. A welcoming host informed her that the seminar was about to start, so she quickly found a seat a few rows from the front.

She wasn't sure what to expect. The event description had sounded promising, but she half-expected a dry, jargon-heavy talk littered with impenetrable tech-speak. What she didn't expect was the speaker.

A man she guessed to be in his mid-fifties, fit and slightly tanned, with hair just beginning to grey, stepped up to the podium. He didn't look like an IT specialist or a software salesperson. He had the relaxed confidence of someone who had lived through what he was about to talk about.

"Good evening," he began, "I'm David."

He gave a brief overview of his career—how, like Meera, he had trained with a large firm, qualified as a Chartered Accountant, and eventually made partner in one of the Big Four firms before leaving in his early forties to start his own practice.

"That was twenty years ago," he said. "The best decision I ever made."

His presentation was unlike anything Meera had anticipated. Rather than a dry lecture, it was a compelling account of how he had embraced technology from the outset—first with accounting software, then cloud accounting, remote data capture, automated reporting, and eventually a full-scale digital transformation.

"The pandemic," he said, "forced the profession to adopt technology at an unprecedented speed. Almost overnight, we moved client meetings to Zoom, used client portals to exchange documents, and transitioned entirely to electronic filings. Even HMRC decided to *Make*

Tax Digital." He grinned at the last remark, earning a few laughs from the audience.

"But all of that," he continued, "is nothing compared to what's coming next. The biggest changes our profession has ever seen are just around the corner. Bigger than the personal computer. Bigger than accounting software. Bigger than cloud accounting."

He explained how the *digital firm* was becoming the dominant business model for modern accountants. Lean, tech-driven, and often fully virtual, these practices would rely on outsourcing, automation, and AI to handle the bulk of traditional accounting work. Large offices filled with staff manually processing transactions would soon become obsolete.

"Digital transformation isn't just about using cloud software," he explained. "It's about integrating technology at every level of your practice—creating seamless workflows from pricing and onboarding to billing and reporting. It's about building a *connected* practice, one that continuously improves efficiency and delivers better client service at a lower cost.

"And here's the real shift—your *clients* will be adopting this technology too. They won't need to pay you to enter transactions or reconcile bank statements when an AI-driven system can do it instantly, 24/7, with no errors, no sick days, and no salary."

The room fell silent.

"But here's the exciting part," he said. "They will need you more than ever—just for a completely different reason. With technology handling the mechanics, businesses will need accountants who can help them *interpret* their numbers. They'll need advisors, strategists, and problem-solvers. The accountant of the future won't be a data processor—they'll be a trusted partner, helping clients navigate growth, risk, and competition."

The host stood up to thank David, and the audience broke into applause.

Meera froze in her seat. She felt a surge of excitement—but also a flicker of doubt. Had she made a huge mistake? Could she really build the kind of practice David had described?

David remained at the front as audience members approached him with questions. Meera hesitated. *I'm not even a proper practice owner yet*, she thought. *Would he even want to speak to me?*

But then she remembered something she had read: *The only silly question is the one you don't ask.*

Taking a deep breath, she walked up to him.

"Hi," she said quickly before she lost her nerve. "I'm Meera, and I'm about to start my own accountancy practice, specialising in working with female entrepreneurs."

David smiled. "Good to meet you, Meera. It's an exciting time to start your own practice."

"I was wondering..." she hesitated, then pushed forward. "I really enjoyed your talk, and I'd love to ask you a few questions. As someone who's built a successful digital practice, could you offer me any advice—or at least point out some pitfalls to avoid?"

Why did I say that? I sound ridiculous!

But if David thought so, he didn't show it. Instead, he laughed.

"Well," he said, "you're clearly determined—I like that. Look, I must run, but if you want to talk, let's meet for a coffee next week. Bring your aspirations—and your toughest questions."

Meera could hardly believe it. Now, as she sat in a quiet corner of the coffee shop, waiting for David, she felt equal parts excited and nervous.

When he arrived, he wasted no time. "Meera, I remember being in your shoes. I've been thinking about what you said—so tell me. Why do you want to start your own practice?"

Meera's heart pounded. This was her chance.

She spoke about her early fascination with business, the evenings spent with her father calculating profit margins, and how that passion led her to qualify as a Chartered Accountant.

"But why leave a secure job for the uncertainty of starting from scratch?" David challenged.

"I don't see it as giving something up," Meera replied. "It's just the next step. My purpose is to empower female entrepreneurs—to give them financial clarity and confidence. My vision is to create a virtual practice that supports women in business with innovative technology and strategic advice."

David smiled. "You've put real thought into this."

Then he leaned forward. "I have strict principles about what makes a successful practice. If you're serious, and agree with them, I might just mentor you."

Meera's mind raced. *What exactly are these 'principles'?* She was about to find out.

Summary of Key Points:

- A pivotal meeting reshaped the author's approach to business.
- Mentorship and fresh perspectives drive better decision-making.
- Small moments can create lasting change when acted upon.

Actions:

1. Identify a key lesson – Reflect on a conversation that shaped your business thinking.
2. Engage with a mentor or advisor for fresh perspectives.
3. Take action – Apply an overlooked lesson to improve your business.

The Seven Principles

Meera took a deep breath as she sat across from David in the quiet corner of the coffee shop. The past few weeks had been a whirlwind—leaving her secure job, setting up her practice, and now unexpectedly getting the chance to learn from someone who had already walked the path she was about to take.

David didn't waste time. "If we work together, our goal will be to build a business that's enjoyable to run, allows you to work the hours you choose, and gives clients the financial insights they need to grow and improve their businesses."

Meera nodded, eager to absorb everything.

"There are seven principles—although I prefer to call them habits—that underpin an effective, successful, and sustainable accountancy practice."

He leaned forward. "These habits separate those who struggle from those who build thriving practices. Let's go through them."

1. Trust Your Intuition

"The first habit is about you, Meera," David began. "You must trust your intuition. That small voice inside you always knows what you should do, even when it doesn't seem logical. It operates in the field of the unknown—and we tend to fear the unknown because we can't predict the outcome. But growth happens outside your comfort zone."

He paused. "People—well-meaning friends and family—will urge you to play it safe. To build something remarkable, you must listen to yourself - be curious, step into uncertainty, feel the fear, and do it anyway."

2. Attract the Right Type of Client

"There are two types of clients," David continued, "transactional clients and relational clients."

"The first type see everything as a transaction. They believe they're the expert and buy based on price alone. The second type—relational clients—see you as the expert and expect you to get to know their business. They are happy to pay the right price and pay on time."

He smiled knowingly. "One of the biggest mistakes accountants make is taking on too many of the wrong clients. When starting out, it's tempting to say yes to everyone. But poor-quality clients drain your time, pay late, and question your fees."

Meera listened intently.

"It's better to have a few high-quality clients rather than too many clients. You started your own practice for financial and time freedom—don't make the mistake of working long hours just to earn a decent income."

3. Establish Your Niche and Identify Your Ideal Client

"You already know you want to work with female entrepreneurs," David said. "That's a great start. Now, you must refine your ideal client persona."

"A big part of growing your practice is being selective about who you take on. You need to identify who fits your ideal client profile—and diplomatically reject those who don't."

Meera frowned. "Reject clients?"

David nodded. "Absolutely. The wrong clients are always unhappy. No matter what you do, they'll blame others - the economy, the government, even the weather - for their failures ." He shook his head. "Don't work with people like that."

4. Charge What You're Worth

"A common trap for new accountants is offering low fees to attract clients – I call this the low-fee mistake."
Meera nodded—she had been thinking about pricing a lot.

"It's tempting to undercharge, especially when you're just starting out. But remember, charging what you're worth, isn't just about money—it's about valuing yourself."

"We give our best when we charge our worth. We prepare better, deliver better, and serve at a higher level." He leaned back. "The right clients don't want cheap advice. Start as you mean to go on. We'll go deeper into pricing when we talk about attracting the right clients."

5. Become a Digital Practice

"Technology has changed everything," David said. "Cloud accounting, automation, and digital tools make you more efficient allowing you to focus on what really matters: helping your clients make better financial decisions."

"Many accountants haven't embraced this change. But those who do are setting themselves apart."

"The more you automate, the more time you have to engage with clients. And with real-time data from cloud accounting, you can offer deeper insights and more strategic advice."

David paused. "Pick one accounting software platform for all your clients. My preference is Xero, but you could also use FreeAgent, QuickBooks Online, or Sage. Keep it streamlined."

6. Define the Scope of Your Services

"Once you've had a discovery call with a prospect, you must define the scope of your services—and stick to it." He gave Meera a sharp look. "Don't let clients dictate what they think they need - you're the expert."

"For example, if a client needs bookkeeping, don't let them do it themselves. Either provide the service, find them a bookkeeper, or outsource it. But don't let them cut corners."

7. Build a Robust Onboarding Process

"First impressions matter," David said. "Once you win a client, their onboarding experience should be smooth and seamless."

"Many firms underestimate this. A poor onboarding process leads to confusion and frustration. A great one builds trust and sets the tone for a long-term relationship."

"These days, onboarding is largely digital—ID checks, software setup, process explanations. But whether in person or online, it must be structured and professional."

David leaned back. "I know that's a lot to take in. But these seven habits will set you apart from the majority of firms."

He looked Meera in the eye. "Take a couple of days to think about each habit. If you're serious, and if you want to build a practice based on these principles, let me know. We'll schedule our first mentoring session."

Meera sat in silence for a moment. She had expected technical advice, maybe some business tips. But this was different. It wasn't just about running an accountancy practice—it was about building the kind of life she wanted. She looked at David and smiled. "I'm in."

Summary of Key Points:

- Seven core principles form the foundation of a successful business.
- Applying these principles ensures financial stability and strategic growth.
- Consistency in execution is key to long-term success.

Actions:

1. Identify your strengths and weaknesses based on the seven principles.

PRACTICE!

2. Choose the principle with the biggest gap and take action.
3. Embed the principles and apply them consistently in daily decision-making.

Regulatory and Compliance Essentials

Meera absorbed everything David had told her about the habits of successful accountants. Some of it had been surprising, but as she worked through each principle, it started to click into place. Now, with their first mentoring session on the horizon, she was eager to get started.

David nodded approvingly. "Good, Meera. But before we go any further, there's a crucial first step we need to cover."

"As a Chartered Accountant running your own practice, you'll be subject to the rules and regulations of several authorities. Each has its own requirements, and compliance is non-negotiable. Some of these can be quite rigorous, but if you set everything up correctly from the outset, you'll save yourself a lot of headaches later on."

Meera leaned forward. "Can you help me work out exactly what I need to do?" she asked.

"Of course," David replied. "Let's break it down."

1. Your Accountancy Body – ICAEW Compliance

"As a Chartered Accountant, you are regulated by The Institute of Chartered Accountants in England and Wales (ICAEW). Their rules require you to hold a **Practising Certificate**, which must be renewed annually. This certificate grants you the authority to use the term 'Chartered' and means you are subject to their Practice Assurance scheme, which allows them to monitor your work and hold you accountable for any shortcomings.

"To obtain your Practising Certificate, you may need a reference from another practising accountant who is also an ICAEW member. One of the partners from your previous firm would be the best person to ask."

2. Anti-Money Laundering (AML) Regulations

"You're probably already aware that accountants fall under the scope of *Anti-Money Laundering (AML) Regulations*. As a practice owner, you must be supervised by an official regulatory body. In your case, ICAEW will automatically become your AML supervisor.

"This means you will also act as your firm's *Money Laundering Reporting Officer (MLRO)*. You'll need to request a letter from the ICAEW confirming their supervisory role, as HMRC may require this before issuing your agent codes** (see section 5)."

David continued, "Additionally, you must obtain a *Disclosure and Barring Service (DBS) basic certificate* to show any prior convictions, police cautions, reprimands, or warnings.

"The AML regulations—formally called the *Money Laundering, Terrorist Financing and Transfer of Funds (Information on the Payer) Regulations 2017* - are extensive. They go far beyond simply verifying client identities. You'll need to create a **Compliance Policies and Procedures Statement** and a **Firmwide Risk Assessment Statement**. Each prospective client must undergo a risk assessment, categorising them as high, medium, or low risk."

Meera frowned. "That sounds like a lot of work."

David nodded. "It is, but ICAEW offers excellent training on AML compliance, and I highly recommend taking advantage of it. You'll have come across much of this in your previous firm's training."

3. Data Protection – The Information Commissioner's Office (ICO)

"In addition to financial regulations, you must also comply with UK data protection laws. These include the *Data Protection Act 2018 (DPA)*, the *UK General Data Protection Regulation (UK GDPR)*, and the *Digital Economy Act (DEA)*.

"These laws require businesses that process personal data to follow strict data protection principles, ensuring that information is:

- Processed for specific, legitimate purposes
- Kept accurate and up to date

- Stored securely and protected from unauthorised access
- Retained only as long as necessary

"You must register your practice with the *Information Commissioner's Office (ICO)* as a data controller, since you'll be collecting and handling client data.

"As your firm's *Data Protection Officer (DPO)*, you must prepare a **Data Protection Policies and Procedures Statement** and a **Privacy Statement**. Most firms publish these on their websites for transparency. Fortunately, the ICO website (ico.org.uk) provides extensive guidance to help you stay compliant."

4. Professional Indemnity Insurance (PII)

"The ICAEW also requires you to have *Professional Indemnity Insurance (PII)*. This ensures that if a client claims against you for professional negligence, you're covered.

"The level of cover depends on your actual or projected fee income, but as a sole practitioner, a typical cover level is £250,000. Several ICAEW-approved insurers offer policies tailored to accountants."

5. HMRC Agent Registration

"To file tax returns on behalf of your clients, you must **register as an agent with HMRC**. This registration applies separately to Self-Assessment, Corporation Tax, VAT, and PAYE.

"These registrations can be completed via the gov.uk website. Be aware that HMRC will request proof of AML supervision before approving your applications."

David paused. "I know this seems like a lot, but getting all of this in place now will make your life much easier in the long run."

Meera took a deep breath. "It's a lot to take in, but I see the importance of setting up correctly from the start. Thanks for walking me through it all."

David smiled. "No problem. We'll go through each step in more detail when you're ready to start implementing. For now, just familiarise yourself with the requirements so nothing catches you off guard."

Summary of Key Points:

- Compliance is critical for accountancy practices to avoid legal and financial risks.
- Key areas include AML regulations, tax filings, GDPR, and professional ethics.
- Staying ahead of regulatory changes ensures client trust and smooth operations.

Actions:

1. Identify and fix any gaps in your regulatory obligations.
2. Monitor legal changes through professional bodies and training.
3. Use software for AML checks, and data security.

MEERA MAPS OUT HER BUSINESS MODEL

Meera was back in her usual seat at the coffee shop, notebook open and ready to dive into the next stage of her business journey. She could barely contain her excitement. "So, am I ready to start getting clients now, David?" she asked eagerly.

"Not quite," David replied with a knowing smile. It was time to define her business model - how she would deliver value to her clients while building a profitable, sustainable firm.

David leaned back, sipping his coffee and said, "Let's start with a question: What do Kodak, Xerox, and Blockbuster have in common?"

Meera thought for a moment. "They were all market leaders who collapsed because they failed to adapt."

"Exactly," David said. "Kodak actually invented the digital camera in 1975, but they shelved it to protect their film business. Blockbuster could have bought Netflix for peanuts but dismissed it as a niche idea. Xerox created game-changing computer technology but ignored it because their photocopying business was too profitable."

"They got comfortable," Meera said, nodding.

"They resisted change," David corrected. "Because they were successful, they assumed they always would be. They didn't think like entrepreneurs."

Meera was beginning to see where this was going.

"An entrepreneur's job is to spot opportunities and act," David continued. "Large corporations have layers of decision-making, bureaucracy, and risk aversion that slow them down. That's why disruptive startups—like Apple in Xerox's case or Netflix in Blockbuster's—take over."

Meera jotted in her notebook: *Don't protect the old, build for the future.*

David smiled. "So, how does this apply to your business model?"

"Well," Meera said, "I can't afford to get stuck in old ways of doing things. If I want to create a digital-first practice, I have to think ahead, not just follow what's been done before."

"Exactly. Your advantage isn't just your technical expertise—it's your ability to adapt. Your clients don't just need compliance work; they need strategic advice, financial clarity, and digital solutions that will help them run better businesses."

"Which is why before you can start to get clients we need to map out your business model and make sure its fit for purpose as a digital practice. Have you heard of the Business Model Canvas?"

"Yes, we had a training session about it at my previous firm," Meera said, frowning slightly. "But to be honest, I didn't think it was that relevant to my work at the time, so I can't say I remember much about it. Why do you ask?"

"Because a business model describes how an organisation—like your accountancy practice—creates and delivers value to its clients. It's essential to define yours before you start attracting clients.

"In fact, many of the decisions you've already made have been shaping your business model without you even realising it. And just as important as deciding what you will do is deciding what you won't do. For example, choosing to be a fully digital practice rules out other options."

David took out his tablet and pulled up an image of the Business Model Canvas — a widely-used framework developed by Alexander Osterwalder and Strategyzer.com. It's available under a Creative Commons licence, which means Meera could freely use it to structure both her business and her clients.

BUSINESS MODEL CANVAS

Key Partners	Key Activities	Value Proposition	Customer Relationships	Customer Segments
	Key Resource		Channels	

Cost Structure	Revenue Streams

"This tool is something I've used with a lot of my clients," he explained. "It ensures you've thought about all the key areas of your business so nothing critical gets overlooked. Let's go through it together."

Meera nodded. "Sounds fun! And I might even be able to use it with my clients in the future." Exactly," said David, who pulled out a sheet of paper and wrote down the key elements of Meera's business model:

1. Customer Segments

Meera already knew she wanted to work with female entrepreneurs, but now she refined it further:

- **Ambitious Female Entrepreneurs** – Scaling their businesses, needing strategic financial guidance.
- **New Female Founders** – Overwhelmed by finances, looking for clarity and direction.
- **Established Business Owners** – Seeking high-level advisory support during growth phases.

2. Value Proposition

"What problem do you solve, Meera?" David asked.

She thought for a moment. "I give female entrepreneurs financial confidence and clarity, using technology to make their businesses more efficient."

"Good," David said. "Now break that into services."

- **Accounting & Tax** – Compliance, planning, and proactive tax strategies.
- **Financial Automation** – Helping clients integrate technology to streamline their finances.
- **Advisory Services** – Cash flow forecasting, business planning, and decision-making support.
- **Education & Community** – Webinars, content, and networking for female entrepreneurs.

3. Delivery Model

Meera's practice would be **100% digital**, with:

- Cloud-based accounting software for real-time financials.
- Virtual meetings to replace in-person consultations.
- AI-driven automation to handle routine bookkeeping.
- A subscription-based model for advisory services, ensuring ongoing support rather than one-off engagements.

4. Revenue Streams

David tapped the table. "How will you make money?"

- **Monthly Retainers** – Fixed-fee pricing for recurring services.

- **One-Off Advisory Work** – Higher-priced strategic planning and financial restructuring services.
- **Workshops & Courses** – Paid resources for clients wanting to upskill.

"Notice anything?" David asked. Meera frowned, then smiled. "None of these depend on billing by the hour."

"Exactly. Time-based pricing is outdated. You're selling outcomes, not hours."

5. Cost Structure

Meera listed her key costs:

- Cloud software subscriptions.
- Outsourced bookkeeping support.
- Marketing and content creation.
- Professional memberships and training.

"It's lean," David noted, "which gives you flexibility. But remember—investing in automation early will pay off in time savings later."

6. Client Acquisition

"How will you attract clients?" David asked.

- **Referrals & Networking** – Connecting with existing contacts and professional groups.
- **Content Marketing** – Blog posts, LinkedIn articles, and lead magnets.
- **Speaking Engagements** – Positioning herself as an expert in finance for female entrepreneurs.
- **Google My Business & SEO** – Ensuring local and online discoverability.

"What makes you different, Meera?" David challenged.

Meera hesitated, then said, "I'm not just an accountant—I'm a financial strategist, and I make it easy for clients by integrating technology into their businesses."

David nodded. "That's your edge. Don't just say you *do accounts*—make it clear that you're helping business owners thrive."

David leaned back. "So, Meera, now you see how everything fits together. The *Business Model Canvas* isn't just a tool - it's the roadmap to building a profitable, efficient, and fulfilling practice."

Meera nodded. "I love how it brings all the pieces together. And I can see how having this clarity now will make it much easier to grow in the right direction."

As they wrapped up, David asked. "So, Meera, what's the takeaway from Kodak, Xerox, and Blockbuster?"

Meera smiled. "Never assume what works today will work tomorrow. The best business models evolve with the future, not cling to the past."

"Exactly," said David. "Now you're truly ready to start attracting clients."

Summary of Key Points:

1. Define your ideal clients and align your services to their needs.
2. A structured pricing model balances profitability and value.
3. Technology and differentiation drive efficiency and competitiveness.

Actions:

- Define your ideal client who you serve best.
- Refine your pricing and services to ensure they maximise your profitability
- Leverage automation to improve efficiency and scalability.

Quality Over Quantity

Meera was starting to realise that running a successful practice wasn't just about winning clients - it was about attracting the *right* clients. David had warned her about one of the biggest mistakes accountants make: saying yes to everyone and ending up overworked, underpaid, and trapped in a business that felt more like a treadmill than a thriving firm.

"You need to be selective," David had told her. "Not all clients are worth having."

At first, this felt counterintuitive - more clients should mean more revenue, right? But David had been firm. "You don't want to spend your life chasing small invoices, dealing with clients who don't respect your expertise, and running yourself into the ground. You'll get nowhere like that.

Instead, focus on a smaller number of high-value clients who pay well, appreciate your input, and take your advice seriously."

The danger of taking on too many clients

She'd seen it before - partners in her old firm drowning under a pile of clients, jumping from one file to the next, always firefighting but never adding value. Rushed work. Missed deadlines. Sloppy errors.

"When you spread yourself too thinly, your efficiency suffers and so does your reputation," David had pointed out.

"Many accountants undercharge just to land a client. It's a trap. Load up on too many low-value clients, and you create an unsustainable workload for very little reward.

You'll work just as hard," David had said, "but for far less money. And when you run the numbers, you'll see most of those clients are barely profitable.

A full roster of demanding, fee-sensitive clients meant relentless pressure, constant emails, and an endless to-do list."

Meera had seen too many accountants burn out, exhausted from long hours and impossible expectations. She wasn't going to be one of them.

David had made a point that stuck with her. "The more clients you take on, the less time you can dedicate to each one. Weak relationships mean they're more likely to leave when a cheaper option comes along."

Meera wanted deeper relationships, not just transactions. She wanted clients who valued her input and stuck around.

The benefits of high-value clients

With fewer clients, she could offer more than just basic services and become a trusted advisor, offering strategic insights rather than just ticking boxes.

High-value clients understood the worth of expert advice—and paid accordingly.

"You'll earn more from one high-value client than from ten low-value ones," David had told her. "And you'll work less to get it. A well-curated client base means fewer last-minute emergencies, fewer unrealistic demands, and a more predictable workload."

Meera wanted to build a practice on her terms—not be at the mercy of every client with an urgent email. Fewer clients meant more time to build real, long-term partnerships. Stronger relationships led to better retention, more referrals, and a practice known for quality over quantity.

Building a high-value client base

Even as she was just starting, she needed to be disciplined about who she accepted.

"You need criteria," David had said. "Who do you want to work with? Who aligns with your expertise?"

Meera made a list:

- ✔ Female entrepreneurs with growing businesses.
- ✔ Valued financial insights, not just compliance.
- ✔ Open to using technology.
- ✔ Willing to invest in expert advice.

If a prospect didn't fit, she'd politely decline.

High-value clients don't just appear. Meera had to attract them—and that meant showing them why working with her was worth it. She wouldn't sell accounting and tax services. She'd sell clarity, confidence, and business growth. "Don't sell tax returns," David had told her. "Sell peace of mind and strategic success."

Streamlining her onboarding process

To reinforce her positioning, Meera needed a seamless onboarding process—one that made it clear she wasn't just another accountant. She'd:

- ✔ Take time to understand each client's business.
- ✔ Set clear expectations from the start.
- ✔ Ensure every client was the right fit before committing.

"Your onboarding process should make it clear you're a strategic partner, not a compliance machine," David had said.

If she wanted to charge premium fees, she had to deliver premium value. That meant staying ahead—on tax law, financial forecasting, business strategy.

"The more value you bring, the more you can charge," David had reminded her.

Phasing out low-value clients

Over time, she'd have to make tough calls. Some prospects wouldn't fit. She'd either refer them elsewhere or adjust her pricing to reflect the value she provided.

"You're running a business, not a charity," David had said. "If a client isn't right, let them go."

For Meera, this was a turning point. Success wasn't about having the most clients—it was about having the right ones.

By prioritising quality over quantity, she could build a practice that was profitable, rewarding, and enjoyable to run.

As she reflected on David's advice, she realised that this approach would give her three things:

- ✔ Financial security—fewer clients, higher fees, greater control.
- ✔ Professional fulfilment—partnering with businesses that valued her expertise.
- ✔ Freedom—to shape her practice on her own terms.

Her next challenge? Attracting high-value clients. Fortunately, David had a plan for that too…

Summary of Key Points:

- Focusing on fewer, high-value clients leads to better relationships and profitability.
- Quality service fosters loyalty, referrals, and long-term growth.
- Overloading with low-value clients reduces efficiency and dilutes impact.

Actions:

1. Focus on high-value clients who align with your expertise.

Practice!

2. Deliver exceptional service rather than spreading yourself too thinly.
3. Avoid taking on clients who don't fit your business model.

Getting Clients

It was time for Meera to turn her attention to attracting clients. She had always excelled in client relationships at her previous firm, but now she needed to build a clientele from scratch.

David had already suggested starting with her network. "Reach out to former colleagues, clients, and friends. Let them know about your new venture. Word-of-mouth is powerful, especially when you offer something distinctive."

But Meera knew that a critical component of her business development would be identifying her ideal client and generating leads from female entrepreneurs she didn't know. This would help her focus her marketing efforts and tailor her services to meet their specific needs.

"David, how do I identify potential clients and in particular my ideal client?"

David explained the process. "Start by creating buyer personas. Think about the characteristics of the clients you enjoyed working with at your previous firm and who benefited most from your services. Here are some steps:

1. Define their demographics:
   - Age, gender, location, and business size.
   - Meera's ideal clients were female entrepreneurs aged 25-50, running small to medium-sized businesses.
2. Identify their pain points:
   - Understand their challenges and what keeps them up at night. What is the biggest problem or pain they are suffering.
   - Meera's previous clients often struggled with financial management and sought clarity and guidance from her, so she decided to concentrate on this.
3. Understand their motivations:
   - What drives them? What are their business goals?
   - Meera though her clients were motivated by growth, efficiency, and financial stability.
4. Communication preferences:
   - How do they prefer to communicate? What platforms do they use?

- Meera found that her clients were active on LinkedIn and preferred email communication for business matters."

The twelve foundation blocks of successful marketing

"The next stage," continued David, "is to understand that there are twelve foundation blocks of successful marketing for an accountancy practice. David listed these for Meera:

1. Your marketing strategy
2. A conversion focussed website and lead magnet
3. An e-mail marketing system
4. A Google Business Profile
5. A LinkedIn profile
6. Facebook and Instagram pages
7. A Knowledge Centre on your website
8. Setting the right pricing strategy
9. Your process for following up leads
10. Tracking the effectiveness of your marketing
11. The creation of marketing assets
12. Your marketing calendar

"You are well on the way to developing your marketing strategy," said David. "by identifying your client personas, the problems they have and how you'll solve them, the results they'll get and how you'll transform their business."

Creating a website and lead magnet

Next, David emphasised the importance of a professional online presence. "Your website is your digital storefront. It needs to be inviting, informative, and easy to navigate.

So, Meera worked with a web designer to create a user-friendly website that showcased her services, testimonials, and contact information. The website included a blog where Meera could share insights and tips, establishing her as an expert in her field.

To attract potential clients, Meera created a valuable lead magnet—a downloadable guide titled *Financial Tips for Female Entrepreneurs to Boost Business Growth*. Visitors to her website could download the guide in exchange for their email address, helping Meera build a mailing list.

An e-mail marketing system

"Your e-mail marketing system is where you build a relationship with the prospects who have signed up to your mailing list. As soon as they've signed up you send them a welcome sequence of emails – five or six emails over a couple of weeks – to start building a rapport with them by giving them something of value.

These emails don't directly sell anything - that's really important. What they do is establish you as an expert and someone they can start to like and trust.

Following the welcome sequence you then start a series of nurture emails – ideally one a week. Occasionally these should include a direct sales message, for example inviting them to attend a webinar or a trial of a service, but the emphasis should remain on building the relationship between you and the prospective client.

The one inviolate rule is that every email must contain a call to action (CTA) such as to book a discovery call.

It is important to remember that not every prospect will be ready to work with you immediately. For some businesses the timing may simply not be right or their pain severe enough yet.

That's why it's important to maintain a relationship with businesses you'd like to work with in the future. Research has shown how long it takes to put faith in working with a new supplier: the answer comes in the form of three numbers **7, 11** and **4.**

Seven is the number of hours' exposure a prospect needs to have had of you to build trust, **eleven** is the number of touchpoints and **four** relates to the number of places – such as an email, a LinkedIn post, a webinar or an event – they have come across you.

Google Business Profile

Google My Business, and its close relative Google maps, are **free** online tools where you can showcase your practice. They have the advantage, particularly for businesses that want local clients, that a prospect searching for, say, *Accountants near me*, will be presented with a map showing the top three accountants geographically nearest to their location. It is also a place where you can ask for reviews from existing clients, post articles and upload images.

LinkedIn

LinkedIn is the premier social media platform for professional businesses such as accountants; creating your profile and *About* section focused on your ideal target client, the problem you solve and the results they'll get from working with you is essential as most prospects will check out your

LinkedIn profile, as well as your website, before contacting you directly.

"LinkedIn is a powerful tool for connecting with your target audience," David advised. "Use it to build your network and showcase your expertise."

Meera created her LinkedIn profile, highlighting her expertise in supporting female entrepreneurs and her unique value proposition. She regularly posted articles and updates on LinkedIn, sharing tips, industry news, and client success stories. These posts helped to position her as a thought leader and attract her ideal clients.

Meera also used LinkedIn to connect with female entrepreneurs and engage with their content. She reached out to potential clients with personalised messages, offering her lead magnet *Financial Tips for Female Entrepreneurs to Boost Business Growth*, and inviting them to schedule a discovery call.

She crafted a personal message explaining her new practice, highlighting her mission to empower female entrepreneurs and the innovative services she offered. She sent it out to her contacts and posted it on her professional social media profiles.

Facebook and Instagram

While not as important as LinkedIn, it is worthwhile having profiles on both Facebook and Instagram and post articles for your ideal clients. These add to the number of places a prospect may come across you and reinforce your presence on them.

Knowledge Centre

In *They Ask, You Answer* Marcus Sheridan introduced the idea of the Knowledge Centre, a place where prospects could find answers to all their questions about working with you before making direct contact. This is usually hosted on your website for which several plugins are available.

Pricing

"David, how should I price my services?" Meera asked. "At my last firm, we used timesheets and hourly rates, but I never felt they reflected the value we provided."

"Great question," said David. "Time-based billing is a relic of the past. In today's digital age, where much of compliance work is automated, pricing should be value driven.

The starting point is to know exactly what you are selling, and conversely what our clients are buying.

Let's start by being clear about what we **don't** sell. We don't sell time. Your clients are not paying to spend time with you! The biggest mistake I see accountants making in the digital age is to believe the myth that the value they provide is somehow linked to the time they spend on their clients' affairs.

Clients don't care how long it takes you to do something - they only care about how you can solve their problems.

This flawed business model of thinking that they're in the business of selling time is the single biggest reason why most sole practitioners don't get to build a practice that gives them financial and time freedom.

Nor are our clients buying their financial statements or tax returns - at least that is not what motivates them to buy. These are merely the byproducts of what they're buying: an outcome, a solution they are looking for and above all peace of mind.

The reality is that your clients are not price-sensitive; they are value-sensitive. If they see more value than what they're paying, they'll buy from you."

How to structure your pricing

"There are four golden rules to pricing your services," said David, "which are:

- Use "investment" rather than "cost" or "fees."
- Charge monthly fixed fees instead of annual ones.
- Offer certainty and choice—clients want transparency.
- Include a guarantee—clients will pay a premium to eliminate risk.

A client can't differentiate one firm from another by the quality of financial statements or tax returns, but they *can* differentiate based on the experience they receive and *how you make them feel*. The price we charge for this should reflect the value that the client is getting.

The other things clients want from you in relation to pricing are **certainty** and **choice**; long gone are the days when 'you can have any colour so long as it's black'. Clients want - and deserve - to know exactly how much your services are going to cost and have input in choosing the level of service they get.

You should also offer a guarantee. Guarantees are powerful and highly valuable to your client who will pay a premium for risk to be taken away. If you are guaranteeing a result you deserve to be paid more and if the client doesn't get the result you promised they would get, would you be comfortable in keeping their money? In reality you're probably giving a guarantee anyway.

You will get much higher fees by offering certainty, choice and a guarantee rather than billing by the hour.

Presenting your price

How you present your price also matters a lot; the table below shows three options along with what is, and isn't, included in each.

Service	Startup	Growth	Premium
Bookkeeping	✓	✓	✓
Monthly bank reconciliation	✓	✓	✓
Monthly management accounts	✓	✓	✓
Monthly debtors report	✓	✓	✓
Quarterly VAT return	✓	✓	✓
Annual accounts	✓	✓	✓
Corporation tax return	✓	✓	✓
Annual budget and cash flow		✓	✓
Monthly/quarterly meeting		✓	✓
Self assessment return		✓	✓
Company secretarial		✓	✓
Quarterly team strategy meeting			✓
Access to training courses			✓
Business mentorship			✓
Investment (per month)	From £250	From £450	From £650

You'll notice that I have used *Investment* rather than cost or fees and quoted the investment as a fixed monthly amount. This has the advantage of being a lot lower than quoting an annual fee but also lets clients spread the cost of your services over 12 months rather than receiving a large bill once a year.

By billing and collecting your fixed fees monthly in advance, you eliminate the need for timesheets, work in progress and debtors."

"That's amazing," said Meera. "I would never have worked all that out for myself. But how do I work out what to charge for one-off projects?

"Another good question," said David. "The key is to work out exactly what the client is looking to achieve and what it will be worth to them when they have achieved it.

Your first decision Is whether to include the work within your fixed monthly fee or whether it is something outside of scope. Quite often you will find that you may want to include just giving advice within the scope of your monthly fee but that implementing the advice becomes outside of scope and incurs an additional fee.

It is then just a question of quantifying the value that the client will get and proposing a fee that is fair for both you and the client for the outcome they will receive."

Follow-up

"Remember the 7, 11, 4 rule?" David reminded her. "That's why you need systematic data capture and a follow-up campaign."

"Not following up is the number one reason accountants fail to convert prospects. Many fear they'll come across as pushy, but the reality is that prospects are busy. They won't remember every email or post."

"The key is to systemise your marketing and business development so you achieve what I call the 'rhythmic acquisition of leads.' Convert leads into prospects, and from those, engage the ones who match your ideal client profile. Then, send them a proposal and book a discovery call."

"And that's what we'll cover next—how to conduct a discovery call that converts a prospect into a client. Another thing many accountants get wrong, as you'll see."

Summary of Key Points:

- Referrals and digital marketing are key channels for attracting new clients.
- Consistency in outreach and follow-up is critical for client acquisition.
- Transparent pricing builds trust and reduces friction in sales conversations.

Actions:

1. Review and action the 12 foundation blocks of marketing
2. Develop a structured approach for outreach, follow-ups, and conversion.
3. **Create clear service packages** and structure service offerings for clients to choose.

THE DISCOVERY CALL

Meera sat across from David, notebook open, pen poised. "David, you always say that selling happens during the discovery call because prospects sell to themselves in their answers. Can we break that down?"

David nodded. "Absolutely. When accountants first engage with a potential client, that initial interaction sets the tone for everything that follows. It's where trust is built, where you demonstrate understanding, and where you set the foundation for a long-term relationship. It's also the moment when you confirm whether a prospect is the right client for you.

"So, the discovery call is more than just a conversation—it's strategic?" asked Meera.

"Exactly. It's about understanding their business, their challenges, their aspirations. You're not just selling a service; you're positioning yourself as the obvious choice to help them achieve their goals. But here's where many accountants get it wrong."

Meera leaned forward. "What are the biggest mistakes?"

"Number one—talking too much," said David. "It's easy to dominate the conversation, especially when you want to prove your expertise. But the goal is to get them talking. Ask the right questions and then listen. The more they talk, the more they reveal."

Meera smiled. "So, silence is a strategy too?"

"More than a strategy—it's essential. And that leads to mistake number two: pitching too soon. You must fully understand their situation before offering solutions. Jump in too early, and you risk missing the real problem."

Meera tapped her pen. "So, it's about patience and timing?"

"Yes. And customisation. That's mistake number three—the one-size-fits-all approach. Every business has its own story. Listen carefully, pick up on their exact words, and tailor your response.

The final mistake? Overselling the 'how.' If you give away too much detail, they either get overwhelmed or they think they can do it without you."

Meera jotted that down. "So, the discovery call should be more about listening, asking good questions, and holding back on solutions until the right moment?"

David nodded. "Exactly. Here's how to structure it. Step one—establish rapport and take control. Open with a friendly greeting, confirm the agenda, and guide the conversation."

"So, I'm leading, but it still feels natural?"

"Yes. Step two—understand their pain. Ask probing questions to uncover what's really going on. Most prospects don't articulate their problems well, so your job is to dig."

Meera nodded. "And then?"

"Step three—understand their business. Get the big picture. Who are their customers? How do they generate revenue? The more context you have, the better your recommendations."

"And then we go deeper into their pain?"

"Exactly. Step four—agitate their pain. Not in a manipulative way, but in a way that makes them realise the cost of not addressing their problems. Then step five—get them to articulate their goals. Where do they see their business in one year, three years, and five years from now? This transition shifts the conversation from problems to solutions."

Meera nodded. "Then we bridge to how we can help?"

"Exactly. Step six—summarise their pain points and ask if they're ready to explore solutions. If they are, move to step seven—secure their commitment. Are they serious about making a change, or are they just fishing for free advice?"

"And then we present our offer?"

"Step eight—explain how you can help but keep it high level. Focus on benefits, not features. Then, step nine—handle their questions and objections. And finally, step ten—explain your pricing with confidence. If you've done everything right, cost won't be a hurdle; it will be an investment in their business."

Meera flipped back through her notes. "So, by the time we discuss price, they already see the value?"

"Correct. And when presenting your services, don't let them cherry-pick. If you let them decide what they think they need, you lose control. Instead, tell them, 'Based on what you've told me, this is what you need. If I were in your shoes, knowing what I know, this is what I'd do.'"

Meera raised an eyebrow. "That's a bold statement."

David smiled. "And that's the point. If you let clients cherry-pick, they'll make poor decisions. But if you confidently prescribe what's best for them, you position yourself as a trusted advisor."

Meera tapped her pen against the table. "So, we shouldn't be afraid to say no if a client asks for something that isn't right?"

"Exactly. Just because you can do something doesn't mean you should. Too many accountants say yes out of fear—fear of losing a client or fear of saying no. But strong businesses are built on offering services that are valuable and profitable, not on bending to every client request."

Meera thought for a moment. "So, compliance isn't dead?"

"Far from it. Whether it's payroll, bookkeeping, compliance, or advisory, every service should stand on its own two feet and be profitable. Plenty of firms do very well in all these areas."

"So, by the end of a good discovery call, the client should clearly see that working with us isn't just an expense—it's an investment in their success?"

"Exactly. And if they're still on the fence, use this killer question: *'The real decision you're making isn't about working with me or someone else. That's irrelevant. The real decision is whether you're ready to take your business where you want it to be. Until you're ready to change, nothing else will make a difference.'*"

Meera leaned back. "That's powerful. It makes them think bigger than just hiring an accountant."

David smiled. "Because we're not just selling services - we're changing lives. Never forget that."

Summary of Key Points:

- A structured discovery call helps assess client fit and uncover pain points.
- Asking the right questions and actively listening builds trust.
- Focusing on value over price improves conversion rates.
- A structured approach filters out unsuitable clients.

Actions:

1. Create a discovery call framework by planning key questions.
2. Show how your services solve problems and deliver results.
3. Write your *killer question*.

GOOGLE BUSINESS PROFILE

"David, should I use Google to get clients?" asked Meera, stirring her coffee thoughtfully.

David smiled. "Good question. Let me ask you something first: when was the last time you looked up a business on Google?"

"Just this morning," Meera admitted. "I was searching for a good café nearby."

"Exactly. And did you scroll past the first few results?"

She shook her head. "No, I picked one from the top three."

"That's the power of Google Maps and Google Business Profile," David said. "And it works the same way for accountants. When someone searches for 'accountant near me,' Google's local search results show a map with three featured businesses. If your practice isn't optimised to rank there, potential clients won't find you."

Meera leaned forward. "So, how do I get my practice into that top three?"

David took a sip of his coffee. "It starts with Google Business Profile. You need to claim and optimise your listing."

"Go to Google Maps and search for your business name. If it's not there, you'll need to add it manually. If it is, claim it by verifying your details. Google usually sends a postcard to your business address with a verification code. Once verified, you can start optimising."

Meera jotted down notes. "What details should I focus on?"

"Everything. Complete every section: business name, address, phone number, website, opening hours, services, and categories. Be specific—as you specialise in small business accounting, tax and advisory services for female entrepreneurs, include that in your categories. Google ranks listings based on relevance, distance, and prominence, so the more complete and accurate your profile, the better."

"Reviews are a major ranking factor," David continued. "The more high-quality reviews you have, the more credible and visible your business becomes. Google prioritises businesses with high rankings and frequent engagement."

"So, I should proactively ask clients for reviews?" Meera asked.

"Absolutely. Provide a direct link to your Google review page to make it easy for them. But here's the trick—guide them. Instead of saying 'Leave a review,' ask them to mention specific services they found valuable. If a client appreciated your cash flow advice, their review should say so. Google picks up on keywords in reviews."

"Many businesses set up their profile and neglect it. Big mistake. Regularly post updates, share articles, and upload images to signal to Google that your business is active. The more engagement your listing receives, the better it ranks."

"Images?" Meera raised an eyebrow. "For an accounting practice?"

"Yes! Pictures build trust. Share images of your home office, client meetings (with permission), or even screenshots of your digital services. Businesses with 100+ images see more clicks and calls than those with fewer."

"Your Google Business Profile is only one part of the equation. Your website needs strong local SEO signals too. Use location-specific keywords—'accountant for small businesses in London' instead of just 'small business accountant.' Also, embed a Google Map on your contact page. It helps Google associate your site with your physical location."

Meera jotted down notes. "And what about backlinks?"

"Essential. Secure links from local directories, industry associations, and even client websites. Google sees these as endorsements, boosting your ranking. If you write guest articles for industry websites, always include a link back to your site."

"Google Business Profile has a section called *Posts*, where you can share updates, special offers, or quick insights. Use it like a mini-blog. It keeps your profile fresh and engaging."

"And what about the Q&A section?"

"Monitor it. Prospective clients can ask questions about your services, and anyone - including competitors - can respond. Monitor it closely and provide clear, professional responses. Anticipate common questions and answer them proactively."

"Finally, track your performance. Google provides insights—how many people viewed your listing, clicked your website, or contacted you. Use this data to refine your strategy. If most searches come from a specific area, focus your marketing efforts there."

Meera looked up from her notes. "If I do all of this, will my practice rank in the top three?"

David grinned. "There are no guarantees, but following these steps will give you a strong chance. Most importantly, you'll be discoverable. If people can't find you, they can't hire you."

Meera nodded, determination in her eyes. "Looks like I've got work to do."

David raised his coffee cup. "Welcome to the digital-first practice, Meera. This is how you grow a business in today's world."

Summary of Key Points:

- A Google Business Profile is essential for client visibility.
- Optimise your profile with accurate and complete details to improves local rankings.
- Request reviews and guide client feedback.

- Regularly update posts, and images to increase engagement and ranking.

Actions:

1. Claim your Google Business Profile and complete all your details.
2. Encourage satisfied clients to leave keyword-rich reviews and respond to all feedback.
3. Post updates, answer questions, and adjust strategies to improve ranking over time.

ONBOARDING
A NEW CLIENT

David leaned back in his chair and looked at Meera. "Today, we're going to talk about onboarding a new client," he said. "I may have mentioned this before, but a robust onboarding process is one of the key success factors for an accountancy practice.

Meera nodded. "So, once the discovery call goes well, this is the next big step?"

"Exactly," David replied. "Onboarding is where promises made in the discovery call become reality. This phase ensures a smooth transition, establishing a strong foundation for the client relationship."

"Got it," Meera said. "So, where do I start?"

David smiled. "With a warm welcome. It's crucial to express gratitude for their trust and set a positive tone.

This isn't just a formality—it reassures them that they've made the right decision by choosing you."

"Something like a personalised welcome email?"

"Yes, and ideally a welcome package too. Introduce them to your team if you have one, outline your services, and guide them on what documents you need from them."

"That makes sense. And then information gathering?"

"Exactly. This is where you go deep into their financial affairs. Get all the necessary documents and details so you can offer them a tailored service. Aside from personal details and UTRs, you need to understand what financial software they use, their bookkeeping practices, and what management accounts or metrics they rely on."

Meera frowned. "I imagine some clients won't have everything to hand."

David nodded. "They won't. That's why I use a checklist I call a Client Data Questionnaire. Every new client fills it in, and it always highlights missing details—like their Companies House authentication code or prior year tax computations. You'll need to get some of this from their previous accountant."

"I see. And what about software? Should I introduce them to Xero straight away?"

"Absolutely," David said. "Client education is a huge part of onboarding. You're not just signing them up—you're guiding them to use the right tools. Show them how to use Xero, set up bank feeds, a receipt capture app, and get them into the habit of reconciling their transactions weekly or monthly. This makes their life easier and your job more efficient."

Meera jotted some notes. "And I suppose clear expectations are key?"

"Vital," David agreed. "Set expectations early—timelines, deliverables, and how you'll collaborate. Make it clear that this is a two-way commitment. If they don't meet agreed deadlines, it affects everything."

"So, if they're slow in sending documents, I push back?"

"Yes. You're setting professional boundaries. Clients who can't follow a simple process are likely to cause you problems down the line."

Meera nodded. "And technology plays a big role in streamlining this, doesn't it?"

"Massively. You need to introduce them to the latest financial tools to make their operations efficient and give them real-time business insights. This is a game-changer."

"And what about ongoing relationship management?" Meera asked.

"That's the next piece," David said. "Onboarding is just the beginning. You need a structured approach to maintaining the relationship. Monthly check-ins, regular updates, and scheduled reviews help keep things on track."

"So, I should have a system in place to monitor how they're doing?"

"Exactly. I provide a monthly financial report, a meeting to discuss the report and any other matters or queries they have, a quarterly business review, and an annual strategic planning session. These touchpoints keep clients engaged and ensure that my services evolve with their needs."

Meera considered this. "And if their business changes, my approach should too?"

"Correct. Business needs shift, and you need to be flexible—whether that's scaling services up or down, introducing new tools, or offering additional advice. Your job is to be proactive."

"And I should ask for feedback regularly?"

"Yes," David said. "Feedback helps you improve. Encourage clients to share their thoughts—both the good and the bad. This shows them you're committed to delivering value."

Meera exhaled. "It's a lot to think about, but it makes sense. So, to summarise, I need to focus on:

1. A warm welcome

    ◌ Personalised email and welcome package
    ◌ Outline services and document submission

2. Information gathering

    ◌ Client Data Questionnaire
    ◌ Financial software, bookkeeping habits, tax details
    ◌ Secure document collection

3. Educational engagement

    ◌ Introductory meeting on goals and challenges
    ◌ Training on financial software and bookkeeping best practices

4. Setting clear expectations

    ◌ Letter of Engagement with scope, timelines, and payment terms
    ◌ Regular updates and milestone tracking

5. Technology integration

    - Software setup and support
    - Secure data migration

6. Building a long-term partnership

    - Ongoing meetings and check-ins
    - Continuous feedback for improvement"

David nodded approvingly. "That's it. And remember, even with the best system, challenges will come up. Clients might delay document submission or struggle with new systems. Your job is to keep communication clear, reinforce the two-way commitment, and offer support while holding firm on expectations."

Meera smiled. "I like that approach—firm but supportive."

"Exactly," David said. "A strong onboarding process lays the foundation for a successful client relationship. When done right, it builds trust, efficiency, and long-term success. Stick to the process, and you'll see the results."

Meera closed her notebook. "Thanks, David. This has been really useful. Time to put it into action."

Summary of Key Points:

- A structured onboarding process sets the tone for a successful client relationship.
- Clear communication and expectations prevent misunderstandings.

- A structured approach improves efficiency and reduces friction for both parties.

Actions:

1. Create an onboarding checklist.
2. Set expectations, define roles, timelines, and responsibilities from the start.
3. Use digital tools to streamline contracts, payments, and document collection.

Getting the Right Tech Stack

David leaned back in his chair, watching Meera battle with a spreadsheet. "You're overcomplicating this."

She sighed. "I just need to get through this reconciliation. It's taking forever."

"That's my point," he said. "Your tech stack should be doing the heavy lifting, not slowing you down.

Your tech stack is the backbone of your accountancy practice. It determines how efficiently you manage client data, streamline operations, automate compliance, and scale your business. The right tools free you up to focus on high-value advisory work instead of getting bogged down in manual tasks.

Think of it like a Formula 1 car," David continued. "You don't win races with a sluggish engine. The right tech stack keeps you in pole position.

A well-structured tech stack automates repetitive tasks, reduces human error, and eliminates inefficiencies. It lets your practice grow without piling on admin costs. More importantly, it enhances client experience—seamless communication, smooth data collection, real-time reporting.

And let's not forget compliance. AML regulations, GDPR, tax laws—non-negotiable. Your tech should help you stay compliant while safeguarding sensitive financial data."

Choosing the right tech for her practice

David folded his arms. "So, what's missing from your tech stack?"

Meera hesitated. "Honestly, I don't even know where to start."

"Then let's break it down. What do you need your software to do?

Before you start grabbing tools at random, identify the core processes that need software support. Every accountancy practice has the same fundamental needs:

Process	Recommended Tools
Accounting & tax	VT Final Accounts, Xero Tax, TaxCalc
AML compliance	Veriphy
Bookkeeping	FreeAgent, QuickBooks Online, Xero, VT

Process	Recommended Tools
Forecasting	Futrli, Spotlight Reporting, Syft
Client communication	Microsoft Teams, Google Meet, Zoom
Data collection	Google Forms, Typeform, Word
Document management	Dropbox, Google Drive, OneDrive
Surveys & feedback	SurveyMonkey, Typeform
Discovery calls	Zoom, Google Meet, Microsoft Teams
Security & backup	Bitdefender, LastPass
Lead magnets	AWeber, ConvertKit, Leadpages
Email marketing	Mailchimp, ActiveCampaign, AWeber
E-signatures	Adobe Sign, DocuSign
Industry updates	HBR, McKinsey, Accenture, The Economist
Payments & invoicing	GoCardless, Stripe
Scheduling	Calendly, Microsoft Bookings
Workflow management	Asana, Monday.com, Trello
Video creation	Camtasia, Loom, Vidyard

You don't need everything on this list," David said. "But you do need the right combination. More isn't always better. If your tools don't integrate properly, you'll spend more time wrestling with them than working.

Integration and automation are critical. Your tools should work together seamlessly, avoiding duplicate data entry and disconnected workflows. Xero integrates with Stripe for payments and GoCardless for direct debits. Trello or Asana can sync with your email marketing tools for automated workflows, while Calendly connects with Zoom for instant meeting scheduling."

"But don't overcomplicate it," he warned. "I've seen firms using both QuickBooks and Xero for no reason. That's like trying to drive two different cars - pointless."

Keeping your tech stack up to date

"Let's say you get this right," David said. "How do you stop it from going stale?"

Meera shrugged. "I guess I'll just add new tools when I need them?"

"Wrong approach. Technology evolves fast. If you want to stay ahead, you need to review your tech stack regularly. Here's how:

- **Annual audits** – Check if each tool still meets your needs.
- **Industry updates** – Stay informed with sources like McKinsey and The Economist.
- **Test new tools** – Keep an eye on innovations that improve efficiency.
- **Monitor costs** – Eliminate redundant subscriptions.
- **Client & team feedback** – Identify bottlenecks and inefficiencies.
- **Security updates** – Ensure software is patched and compliant.

"Look," David said, "your tech stack can be your biggest advantage or your biggest headache. If you get it right, you'll save time, ensure compliance, and improve client service. And you'll be able to scale without drowning in admin."

"And if I get it wrong?" Meera asked.

"Then you'll spend half your life fighting with software instead of running your firm. So, audit what you've got, choose wisely, and keep it updated. You remember my presentation—digital-first isn't optional anymore. It's the foundation of a modern accountancy practice. Build your tech stack wisely, and it'll be your most powerful tool for growth."

Summary of Key Points:

- The right technology improves efficiency, accuracy, and client experience.
- Cloud-based tools enable seamless collaboration and remote work.
- Automation reduces manual tasks, freeing up time for higher-value work.

Actions:

1. Assess your current tools, identify gaps in efficiency and areas for improvement.
2. Adopt cloud-based solutions to ensure flexibility, security, and accessibility.
3. **Choose scalable software** that grow with your business and integrate smoothly.

AI and the Power of Prompting and Automation

Meera had heard the phrase countless times recently: '*AI won't take your job, but those who use AI will.*' *The thought unsettled and intrigued her in equal measure.*'

"David, in your presentation a few weeks ago I remember you saying that given the growing importance of AI, any digital transformation should also be an AI transformation, but how do I achieve that?" she said

David leaned in, a knowing smile on his face. "Let's unpack that," he said. "AI isn't just about making tasks faster or cheaper. It's about stepping outside your comfort zone and imagining what hasn't been done before. The real advantage isn't in efficiency alone—it's in the mindset shift it forces us to make."

Meera nodded, though she wasn't entirely convinced.

"The problem is," David continued, "most people interact with AI through the lens of old habits. They ask predictable questions and get predictable answers. But if we want AI to truly unlock new possibilities, we need to rethink how we use it. That's why I ask myself, 'WWAID?'—What Would AI Do?"

Meera frowned slightly, intrigued.

"By treating AI as a partner in thinking, rather than just a tool, we start uncovering ideas we might never have considered," David explained. "The key shift is moving from *'Tell me what I already know'* to *'Show me what I haven't considered yet.'* That's where the magic happens."

She sat up straighter. A recent Harvard Business Review article had outlined ways to train our minds for broader, more creative outcomes with generative AI.

David nodded approvingly. "Let's walk through those ideas," he said. "They might just change the way you approach problem-solving."

1. Establish a daily exploratory prompting habit

Each morning, Meera decided she would challenge herself with an open-ended question: What if I've completely overlooked a key trend in my industry? Sometimes the answers surprised her. Often, they revealed opportunities she hadn't considered.

2. Use 'What if' and 'How might we' questions

Instead of asking, *How do I improve productivity?* she'd reframe it: *What if I abandoned all my usual tactics? What new approach might emerge?* The shift encouraged fresh thinking.

3. Embrace ambiguity and curiosity

David reminded her, "Don't rush to a neat conclusion." When Meera asked: *What might I be overlooking in my pricing strategy?* AI offered angles she hadn't expected.

4. Use AI to explore, not just solve

Rather than seeking a quick fix, she'd pose bigger questions: *What if AI had a seat at my practice's boardroom table - how would it shape decision-making?* The answer was a wake-up call about the future of delivering client service.

5. Chain prompts together to evolve ideas

When AI suggested a new product feature, she'd follow up with: *How would this evolve in five years?* Step by step, her concept moved from good to visionary.

6. Think metaphorically

David encouraged her to see problems differently. She once prompted AI with: *"Imagine my marketing plan as a garden—how should I tend it?* The metaphor unlocked new growth strategies.

7. Seek multiple perspectives

She asked: *How would an artist, a scientist, and a philosopher each approach this challenge?* The range of responses widened her field of vision.

8. Experiment with role-playing prompts

Meera asked AI to think like Steve Jobs, Walt Disney, or a visionary CEO. Each persona provided a unique angle, stretching her beyond her usual thinking patterns.

PRACTICE!

9. Ask for impossibilities

'*Show me solutions that would make my business completely obsolete,*' she once prompted. It was counterintuitive, but it highlighted blind spots in her strategy that she had never considered.

10. Reimagine AI's role in solutions

David posed a challenge: "Don't just use AI—ask AI how it would solve the problem if it had full freedom." She tried it, and the results were unlike anything she could have predicted.

11. Set a weekly 'future-driven' prompt session

She decided to schedule time to explore long-term trends. '*Where will my industry be in ten years?*' Asking this regularly kept her ahead of the curve.

12. Keep a record of breakthrough prompts in your journal

She'd record the prompts that led to unexpected insights. Reviewing them would help her refine her thinking over time.

 Through this process, Meera came to understand something profound: Generative AI isn't just a tool - it's a catalyst for expanding how we think. The real breakthroughs come when we stop treating AI as an answer machine and start using it as a thought partner.

 But more than that, she realised that the most powerful shift wasn't in the AI itself—it was in her mindset. Curiosity and bold questions sparked responses she never saw coming.

"Is there a better way?" David often asked. That simple question forced her to challenge her default assumptions, push beyond surface-level solutions, and explore opportunities others might miss entirely.

"So, David, how can I use AI to make my practice more profitable?" Meera asked, leaning forward with curiosity.

David smiled. As you've just seen Meera AI is going to cause a fundamental shift in how accountancy practices operate. If you embrace it properly, AI—especially tools like ChatGPT—can transform your accountancy practice by automating repetitive tasks, improving decision-making, and unlocking new revenue streams."

"One of the biggest drains on profitability in an accountancy practice – particularly when you are a sole practitioner - is time spent on repetitive, manual tasks," David explained. "AI can help streamline these processes. Think of ChatGPT as an intelligent assistant that can handle many of the mundane activities that slow you down. I often say that ChatGPT is your best friend when it comes to saving you time by doing:

- Email drafting & communication: ChatGPT can generate client emails, summarise lengthy correspondences, and adjust the tone for different audiences.
- Client onboarding: AI chatbots can answer common client questions, reducing the need for manual responses.
- Data entry and expense categorisation: AI can sort and categorise financial transactions quickly, reducing human error.

- Document summarisation: AI can analyse financial reports and extract key insights, saving hours of manual review.

Meera nodded. "So, instead of spending hours on admin, I can focus on higher-value work?"

"Exactly. Freeing up your time means you can spend it where it matters most - advising clients and growing your business. Because AI isn't just about automation. It can make you a smarter, more informed advisor," David continued. "You can use it for:

- Predictive financial modelling: AI can analyse historical data to forecast cash flow trends, helping clients make better decisions.
- Spotting problems early: AI tools can scan financial statements for anomalies and flag potential issues before they become problems.
- Industry-Specific insights: AI can generate tailored business advice based on sector trends, giving clients a competitive edge."

Meera's eyes widened. "So, AI can actually help me provide better insights to my clients?"

"That's the real power of AI," David confirmed. "With AI-powered tools, you can go beyond traditional number-crunching and offer strategic guidance.

Nor is AI just for internal efficiencies - it can also help you attract and retain clients," David said. "AI can create content for marketing, generate blog posts, LinkedIn updates, and even video scripts. It can analyse client data to tailor marketing messages based on individual needs as well as can generate customised financial reports, to make complex data easier for clients to understand.

Meera smiled. "If AI can help with marketing, that's a game-changer."

"It absolutely is," David agreed. "With AI, you can maintain visibility in your market without spending endless hours on creating content."

"But AI won't work unless your practice is structured for it," David cautioned. "Here's what you need to do first:

- Clean, structured, and accessible data is key to AI's effectiveness.
- Start small—use ChatGPT for email drafting and content creation, then expand into automation and client insights.

Meera took a deep breath. "This sounds like the future of accounting."

David nodded. "And the firms that embrace AI early will have a significant advantage. The question is—are you ready to lead the way?"

She looked forward to her journey with a sense of optimism. The future was still uncertain, but now, equipped with the right questions, she was ready for it. And as David often reminded her, "AI won't take your job. But the person who knows how to think with AI? They just might."

Summary of Key Points:

- AI is not just about automation; it transforms the way accountants think and work.

- The biggest breakthroughs happen when AI is treated as a thought partner.
- AI can automate repetitive tasks, freeing you to focus on high-value advisory services.

Actions:

1. Develop a habit of asking AI open-ended, exploratory questions.
2. Apply AI to enhance strategic thinking, decision-making, and advisory capabilities, not just for automation.
3. Use AI as a mentor, a consultant, or a board member in decision-making simulations.

Setting up her Home Office

One of Meera's first realisations was that her workspace was just as important as the technology she used. She needed an environment that fostered productivity, efficiency, and focus. So, she turned to David for guidance.

"David, what do I actually need to set up a home office that works for a digital accountancy practice?" she asked.

David nodded knowingly. "That's a great question, Meera. Too many people overlook this part, but your working environment plays a crucial role in your success. You want a setup that allows you to work comfortably and efficiently while minimising distractions. Your office should be a space where you can focus, take breaks when needed, and feel at ease."

Practice!

He leaned forward. "Here's what I recommend you invest in to create the ideal home office setup."

Essential furniture and equipment

Ergonomic Chair	A supportive chair is non-negotiable. You'll be spending long hours at your desk, and a good chair will prevent back and neck pain. Think of it as an investment in your health, not an expense.
Desk	A spacious desk with enough room for your computer, monitors, and essential documents.
Lighting	Proper lighting reduces eye strain. Natural light is ideal, but an adjustable LED desk lamp works well too.
Storage Solutions	A filing cabinet or well-organised storage system to keep paperwork and office supplies in order.
Bookshelves	A dedicated space for your business and technical reference books.

Technology and tools

Laptop or Desktop	A powerful computer is a must. A laptop offers flexibility, while a desktop may be more efficient if you work from one location.

Monitor	A high-resolution screen or dual monitors can significantly improve productivity by making multitasking easier.
Keyboard & Mouse	Ergonomic options can prevent wrist strain and improve comfort.
Printer/Scanner	A multifunctional device is useful for handling documents that require signatures or physical copies.
High-Speed Internet	Fast, reliable internet is crucial for cloud-based accounting and video calls.
VOIP Phone & Mobile	A business phone line for professionalism, with a mobile for when you're on the move. A dual SIM phone can help separate personal and business calls.
Webcam, Microphone & Headphones	Essential for virtual meetings. A high-quality webcam and noise-cancelling headphones can make all the difference.

Software & digital tools

Xero Accounting Software	Your go-to accounting software for managing client finances and real-time collaboration.
Project Management Tools	Trello or Asana help keep track of client tasks and deadlines.

Communication Tools	Zoom or Microsoft Teams ensure seamless virtual meetings.
Document Management	Google Workspace or Microsoft 365 for cloud storage and document collaboration.
Scheduling Software	Calendly allows clients to book appointments without endless email back-and-forth.

Cybersecurity & backup

VPN (Virtual Private Network)	A secure internet connection is essential for protecting client data.
Antivirus Software	Keeps your computer safe from malware and cyber threats.
Backup Solutions	Use an external hard drive or cloud storage like Dropbox for regular data backups.
Surge Protector	Protects your devices from unexpected power surges.

David leaned back. "This setup will create an efficient and comfortable working environment, allowing you to focus on building your practice without distractions."

He then added with a serious expression, "One more thing, Meera. We need to discuss your personal safety. As a single female working from home, you should take precautions to protect yourself. I won't go into it now, but I'll send you some thoughts via email."[1]

---

[1] A copy of David's email is in the Resources section at the back of this book.

With her workspace coming together, Meera turned her attention to optimising her workflow. She knew she needed efficient processes to keep up with an increasing workload.

"David, I need to make sure I'm working smart. What should I focus on?" she asked.

David smiled. "Automation is your best friend. The more you can automate, the more time you'll have for high-value tasks like client advisory and business growth. Let's walk through some key areas."

Streamlining your processes

1. Automating invoicing & payments – Xero can handle automated invoicing, payment tracking, and reminders, reducing manual work and late payments.
2. Using project management tools – Asana helps you create client-specific projects, set deadlines, and track progress. It keeps everything organised and on schedule.
3. Integrating communication tools – Scheduling regular Zoom check-ins with clients keeps communication consistent and eliminates misunderstandings. Document management – Microsoft OneDrive ensures all documents are stored securely, accessible anytime, and updated in real time.

Meera took notes, already envisioning how these changes would make her practice more efficient.

David concluded, "Your goal is to work smarter, not harder. The right systems will allow you to scale your practice without feeling overwhelmed."

Meera nodded, feeling more confident than ever. She was no longer just preparing to start her practice—she was actively building it.

Summary of Key Points:

- A well-designed home office boosts productivity and professionalism.
- The right technology and tools ensure efficiency and seamless client communication.
- Separating work and personal space helps maintain focus and boundaries.

Actions:

1. Optimise your workspace and create a dedicated, clutter-free area for focus.
2. Invest in technology – use reliable hardware, software, and communication tools.
3. Set clear routines to separate work and personal life.

The First 90 Days

Meera sat at her desk, staring at the business plan she'd made following her meetings with David. It had been a whirlwind of preparation - setting up systems, refining her ideal client profile, and crafting her service offering. Now, the real challenge began. The first 90 days would determine everything.

David's voice echoed in her head. 'Your first three months in business aren't about making money; they're about building strong habits. Get this right, and success will follow.'

The first thing Meera did was map out her top priorities:

- ¤ Client acquisition: Secure her first five ideal clients.
- ¤ Revenue milestones: Generate a sustainable monthly income.

- Process development: Implement efficient workflows for client onboarding, service delivery, and financial tracking.

Clarity was key. Without it, she'd waste time chasing distractions instead of focusing on what truly mattered. David had been blunt: '*A business without clear goals is just wishful thinking.*'

Success wasn't about working harder—it was about working smarter. Meera established daily habits to drive productivity and growth:

- Morning strategy session: Review key priorities and plan the day.
- Dedicated client hours: Set specific time blocks for client work, avoiding multitasking.
- Business development time: Every day, she dedicated 60 minutes to marketing and outreach—because clients wouldn't just appear.
- Financial check-ins: Weekly reviews ensured cash flow stayed healthy and expenses remained under control.

David had warned her: '*Many businesses fail because they focus on the wrong things. Do what drives revenue first—always.*'

And with no boss to dictate her schedule, Meera had to become her own best manager. That meant:

- Prioritising High-Value Tasks: She focused on work that directly contributed to business growth, not just admin tasks that felt productive.

- Time Blocking: She scheduled deep work sessions for key projects and client calls, ensuring uninterrupted focus.
- Setting Boundaries: No checking emails every five minutes. No back-to-back meetings. No endless social media scrolling.

Time was her most valuable asset—she refused to waste it.

Starting a business could be isolating. But Meera knew she didn't have to do it alone. She joined professional networks and engaged with like-minded entrepreneurs. Surrounding herself with experienced professionals accelerated her learning and provided much-needed motivation.

- Mastermind Groups: Weekly accountability calls kept her focused.
- Industry Forums & Networking Events: Opportunities to connect, learn, and find new clients.
- Mentorship: Regular check-ins with David to discuss progress and roadblocks.

David had put it simply: *'The right people make all the difference. Find them.'*

Setbacks were inevitable. Meera had already faced moments of doubt, but she had made a decision—she would view challenges as opportunities, not obstacles.

- Resilience: She wouldn't let small failures derail her progress.
- Continuous learning: Regularly reading industry updates, attending webinars, and staying ahead of trends.

- Confidence: Owning her expertise and positioning herself as a trusted advisor.

David's words were clear: *'The most successful business owners aren't the smartest—they're the most adaptable.'*

She had seen too many accountants burn out from overwork and stress. She was determined not to follow that path.

- No working late every night or saying yes to every client request.
- Scheduling downtime: rest was a non-negotiable part of her strategy.
- She'd adjust her workload before reaching breaking point.

Success meant nothing if she was exhausted. Sustainability was the goal.

As Meera looked over her plan, she felt a sense of control. The next 90 days would be tough, but she was ready. She had the knowledge, the strategy, and the mindset to make it work.

David had given her one final piece of advice: 'Act every single day. Small steps compound into big results. Show up, do the work, and trust the process.'

She took a deep breath, opened her laptop, and got to work.

Summary of key points

- Your first 90 days set the foundation for long-term success.

- Prioritise the right tasks to prevent wasted time and resources.
- A strong support network provides guidance, accountability, and motivation.

Actions:

1. Focus on client acquisition, revenue targets, and efficient workflows.
2. Structure daily routines by using time blocking and prioritisation to stay productive.
3. Leverage a support system: engage with mentors and join industry groups.

Resources

What's more important than your life?

Last Thursday I had lunch with three of my best friends and as usual our conversation went on long into the afternoon. At one point Sarah said something that surprised me: many of her similarly middle-aged friends and acquaintances didn't know what they wanted to be when they grew up!

My other friends agreed. Apparently, it is common for people to reach middle age without defining what they want from life. The demands of everyday life - the here and now - overwhelm us leaving little time to think about the long term and what we are working toward. As a result, when faced with big and small life decisions, we are left with nothing to guide us.

The business equivalent, of course, is attempting to run a business without a strategy, which as every business owner knows is a losing proposition.

So, is the model for strategic thinking that we use with businesses suitable for the design of life strategies for individuals?

PRACTICE!

At the Boston Consulting Group, they think so. They have devised a programme they call **Strategise Your Life** that takes the corporate strategy model and adapts it to help individuals. The programme involves asking seven questions:
1. How do I define a great life?
2. What is my life purpose?
3. What is my life vision?
4. How do I decide where to invest my time (BGC calls this your life portfolio because they use their acclaimed product portfolio analysis matrix as an assessment tool)?
5. What studies can I learn from to set benchmarks for life satisfaction?
6. What portfolio choices (ie what if I change my priorities) can I make?
7. How can I ensure and measure a successful and sustained change?

From Corporate Strategy to Life Strategy

The questions that organizations use to set a course for the future can be easily adapted to help individuals do the same.

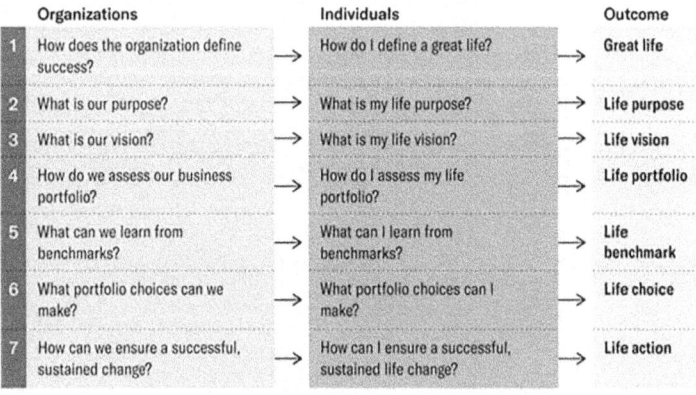

Source: Analyses by Rainer Strack, Susanne Dyrchs, and Allison Bailey ©HBR

94

They argue that just as corporate strategy is a set of choices that positions a business to win, life strategy is a set of choices that positions a person to live a great life. They apply tools from classic business and organisational strategy to help individuals find answers to the seven questions above and make better decisions about their life actions.

These tools help individuals to find their path in a seven-step life strategy process. In step one you define what a great life means for you, in step two you outline your purpose and then in step three your life vision. Step four is the analysis of how you spend your 168-hour week, while step 5 involves setting benchmarks for your level of life satisfaction. In step six you incorporate the results of the first five steps and determine your choices and the changes you are going to make in your life, then in step seven you map out a plan for putting your choices into action.

That said, it won't be easy. You will have to challenge yourself and face your fears. You may have to accept the need to step outside your comfort zone.

But after all, what's more important than your life? Commit to thinking strategically about it, look forward to the insights you will gain and enjoy the journey.

The Seven Steps

The process begins with a simple yet profound question:

1. How do I define a great life?

The starting point of any corporate strategy process is to define the metrics for success. For example, does the business want its strategy to focus on driving sales, profitability or shareholder value?

What are the right metrics in an individual's life? Social norms might suggest we measure money, fame, and power. But studies have shown that money leads to greater happiness only to the extent that our basic needs are met. Recently, a study that has followed residents of inner-city Boston since the 1970s found that meaningful relationships were the key driver of long-term happiness. The late Harvard Business School professor Clayton Christensen agreed: In his classic HBR article "How Will You Measure Your Life?" he wrote, "I've concluded that the metric by which God will assess my life isn't dollars but the individual people whose lives I've touched."

The PERMA model, introduced by Martin Seligman, the founder of positive psychology and a University of Pennsylvania professor, in his 2011 book, *Flourish* and later developed it into PERMA-V, which stands for Positive emotions (frequent feelings of pleasure and contentment), Engagement (being in the flow, losing track of time), Relationships (mutual feelings of caring, support, and love), Meaning (contributing to making the world a better place), Achievement (striving for success or mastery, reaching goals), and Vitality (being healthy and energetic) is one way to determine what makes a great life for you. Start with each element in PERMA-V, or even add your own categories, such as autonomy or spirituality then rate each one's importance to you on a scale from 0 (not important) to 10 (very important). Try to recall periods of deep satisfaction in your past and consider what triggered them.

In strategy projects, I conduct a diagnostic analysis I call Now-Where-How to establish where is business is now – a line in the sand if you like. So, rate your current satisfaction with each dimension on a scale from 0 (not at all satisfied) to 10 (very satisfied). This quick assessment will give you a rough idea of how you define a great life and initial ideas about what you need to change.

2. What is my life purpose?

The two most important days in your life are the day you are born and the day you find out why. —Mark Twain

For a corporate strategy to be successful, it must be anchored to the business's purpose; this is a combination of:

- What are we good at?
- What does the world need with which we can help?
- What are our values?
- What excites us?
- Where can we have the most impact on others?

Using the answers to these questions businesses develop purpose statements. The same questions can be used to find your life purpose. Ask yourself,

- What am I good at? Think about situations at work or in other areas of life in which you have demonstrated critical strengths such as creativity, teamwork, or analytical skills.
- What are my core values? Think about critical decisions you've made and principles you hold dear that have provided direction, such as honesty, fairness, or integrity.
- Which activities am I passionate about? Perhaps your answers include mentoring, problem-solving, or helping young people.

- What need can I help address in the world? It could be one of the 17 Sustainable Development Goals of the United Nations, such as quality education, decent work and economic growth, or innovation.
- Where can I have the most impact on others? Don't try to solve all the world's problems on your own; identify those areas where you can make the most difference.

In the purpose-defining stage of strategy projects, we conduct belief audits: do the same. Ask friends or family members what your strengths are, what values you live by, what things excite you, and what need you might help fill. Draw from your own answers and theirs to draft your purpose statement.

There are other methods for defining one's life purpose, of course. But it's important to find the time and a way to do it. Purpose guides your life strategy.

3. What is my life vision?

The next step in building a corporate strategy is to set out a vision for the future. We typically ask business owners where they want their business to be — in terms of innovation, growth, product portfolio, market presence, etc. — in five to 10 years' time.

So, ask yourself: What story would I like people to tell about me five to 10 years from now? What would I do if money wasn't an issue? What will the 80-year-old me not want to have missed in life? Your purpose and your strengths might also trigger some ideas about your vision.

In both business and individual life strategy, a vision can give you focus. You might end up with a short list of bullet points or a one-sentence summary of your vision. No matter how you capture it, a vision statement can be powerful in guiding your life.

4. How do I decide where to invest my time?

In the 1970s and 80s businesses used the Boston Consulting Group growth-share matrix (also called (product portfolio analysis) to assess their business's products on key parameters such as market growth or share and to decide where to invest capital. BCG is well-known for its 2×2 growth-share matrix.

But what is the equivalent of a business product in life? The answer is to focus on six strategic life areas (SLAs):

- Relationships.
- Body, mind, and spirituality
- Community and society
- Career, learning, and finances
- Interests and entertainment; and
- Personal care.

BCG then subdivide the six SLAs into 16 strategic life units (SLUs) as follows:

Practice!

The Key Areas of Life

People spend their time, energy, and money in six strategic life areas, which can be subdivided into 16 strategic life units. Think about how much time you currently spend on each and rank both its importance and the satisfaction it gives you using a 0–10 scale.

Strategic life areas	Strategic life units	Descriptions
1. Relationships	Significant other	Time with partner, dates
	Family	Engaging with kids, parents, siblings
	Friendship	Time with friends
2. Body, mind, and spirituality	Physical health/sports	Exercise, physical therapy
	Mental health/mindfulness	Psychotherapy, meditation
	Spirituality/faith	Religious practice
3. Community and society	Community/citizenship	Membership in local clubs, jury duty
	Societal engagement	Volunteering, activism
4. Job, learning, and finances	Job/career	Work
	Education/learning	Classes, training
	Finances	Planning, investing
5. Interests and entertainment	Hobbies/interests	Reading, collectibles
	Online entertainment	Social media, TV, gaming
	Offline entertainment	Vacations, theater, sporting events
6. Personal care	Physiological needs	Eating, sleeping
	Activities of daily living	Commuting, housework

Source: Analyses by Rainer Strack, Susanne Dyrchs, and Allison Bailey ©HBR

Look back at the past year and assess how much time you spent on each of the 16 SLUs in an average week. Next, rate all 16 SLUs on a scale of 0 to 10 based on how important they are to you. Then rate the satisfaction you derive from each on the same scale. (This goes one level deeper than the similar PERMA-V exercise.)

Now sketch out your own 2×2; we call it the Strategic Life Portfolio. But instead of mapping growth against share, you will put the importance of each SLU on the y-axis and the satisfaction it brings on the x-axis. Plot each SLU with a bubble, making the size of the bubble roughly proportional to the percentage of time in a week you spend on it.

In the top-left quadrant, you will find the SLUs of high importance and low satisfaction. These are areas of high urgency, because you care about these activities deeply but aren't focusing on them enough to get the most out of them. The SLUs in the top-right quadrant also deserve some attention: You want to keep devoting significant time and energy to your most important and highest-satisfaction activities and invest less in those that are less important (bottom left and right).

Finally, look at your entire 2×2 and ask yourself: Does my current portfolio of SLUs put me on the right track to support my purpose and achieve my vision? Does it bring me closer to how I define a great life? Where can I save and reallocate my time? Just as in corporate strategy projects, you want to set some high-level priorities — rather than a detailed plan — for investments of your time, energy, and money.

5. What studies can I learn from to set benchmarks for life satisfaction?

In almost every strategy project, we do a best practice and benchmarking analysis to understand what we can learn from leading businesses and competitors. We can do the same for individuals by looking at role models and then, more importantly, at the research on life satisfaction.

Ask yourself: Who conducts their personal and professional life in a way I admire? What makes them admirable, and what choices would they make if they were in your shoes?

Now consider what scientific studies tell us about life satisfaction. One of the largest studies on life satisfaction found that significant others, children, friends, sports, spirituality, community involvement, and nutrition all contribute to life satisfaction. Not surprisingly, health problems have a very negative impact. Other studies have found that proven life-enhancers include practicing kindness, mindfulness, meditation, and gratefulness; cultivating more humour and laughter; dedicating time to learning; and developing a growth mindset.

6. What changes in my priorities can I make?

Corporate strategy is about making choices between options: Should we keep our current portfolio, diversify, focus, acquire a company, or enter a new market? In life, the equivalent questions are: What happens if I continue to live my life the way I am now? What if I change my priorities? Equipped with your definition of a great life, your purpose, your vision, your SLU ratings, and your benchmarks, you are ready to find out.

Go back to the great-life exercise in step 1 and think about what you can do for your areas of dissatisfaction. Review your purpose and vision from steps 2 and 3. Think about the SLUs that step 4's portfolio exercise identified as needing more attention, and how you can improve satisfaction or reallocate time there. Then consider how the insights gleaned from step 5's benchmarks can help you with all the above. From this long list of potential changes and actions — small and large — select several that will best move you toward a great life and commit to them.

Be specific about what you want to change. You have only 168 hours each week, which means you must reduce, outsource, or bundle existing activities, or make them more efficient through productivity strategies and tools. For example, when you work out with your significant other or volunteer for a good cause with your friends, you are bundling sports and significant other or societal engagement and friendship.

Life strategy is about setting priorities; it is not about filling every waking minute. Remember to reserve space in your calendar for downtime as well. Researchers have found that people are happiest when they have two to five hours of free time each day.

Remember that even a small change can have a big impact in two key ways. For example, research has shown that doing just 15 minutes of physical activity a day increases life expectancy by three years (despite amounting to only about half a year of time investment). Exercise also gives you a dopamine boost, improving your mood, which benefits those around you and makes you more productive at work, potentially leading to new outputs that greatly impact the lives of others.

If you know which strategic life unit needs work but don't know what changes to make, dig deeper and develop a strategy for that unit — a job/career strategy, a family strategy, a mental health/mindfulness strategy, and so on — just as a business does with its corporate strategy.

For example, to develop a job/career strategy, ask yourself the following questions: How does my current job support my purpose and vision? Does my current job give me a sense of achievement and engagement (two of the six great-life dimensions)? How does my current job align with the strengths I identified in the purpose step? The answers to these questions will give you an idea of how to move forward in your career.

7. How can I ensure and measure a successful, sustained life change?

Change is not easy. Many businesses ensure successful implementation of the strategies they've outlined by using OKRs (Objectives and Key Results). OKRs are focused, ambitious, output-oriented, flexible, measurable, and transparent, and were first introduced by venture capitalist John Doerr in his book Measure What Matters.

I recommend doing the same for each of the changes you committed to in step 6. Define the objectives and the date by which you want to achieve them. Then break down each of those objectives into a few key results or action items, again with deadlines. Consider adding them directly to your calendar.

There are many ways that businesses hold themselves to OKRs.
- *Anchoring* means sharing your plan, as Google does by making its OKRs public. Who will you tell about your plan or ask to join you on your journey?
- *Consequences* means setting up incentives for achievement, such as bonuses for success or penalties for failure. How will you reward yourself when you've successfully changed an aspect of your life, and what will the consequences be if you don't? and
- *Check-ins* means routinely stepping back, refining and adjusting your efforts, and celebrating your

achievements. When each week can you spend 15 minutes to review and update your life strategy?

Your One-Page Life Strategy

Often, the seeming enormity of an important task — like life strategy development — is what stops us from doing it. So, to make what seems impossible possible, I recommend putting your entire life strategy on a single sheet of paper.

To start, write down what defines a great life for you. Next, record your strengths, your values, what lights you up, and what the world needs, and then add your purpose statement that incorporates those ideas. Third, summarise your life vision. Fourth, note the SLUs that are high priorities for action or that you spend too much time on. Next, write down the changes you'd like to make and commit to. Finally, for each of those changes, list an objective and two to three key results with deadlines, and then note the anchors, the consequences, and the check-in plan to make the change stick.

This page is your first minimum viable life strategy. As with corporate strategy, it needs to be reviewed, adjusted, and updated on a regular basis. In addition to your weekly 15-minute check-in, I recommend scheduling a longer, one- to two-hour review session with yourself, (or with a life strategy group you start with other people) every six to 12 months. Review all seven steps, consider setbacks or shifting circumstances, and adjust accordingly.

One couple I know, who wanted to develop life strategies in tandem, went so far as to document their life purposes and goals with photos and notes in a picture frame.

PRACTICE!

They hung it on the wall of their home, a daily reminder of where they want to go both together and as individuals.

Life is full of adventure and trauma, love and sadness, joy and stress. It can be great or terrible. There will be ups and downs. But a lot of it depends on you and the choices you make. A life strategy will not only guide you but also build your resilience so that you're better able to recover from missteps.

Now, go and do the same. Your life is your top strategic priority.

Example of a personal profile

This is an example of a personal profile you can write to set out your goals, purpose, vision and core values.

About Meera

Background and Journey

Hi, I'm Meera, a dedicated and passionate chartered accountant in my 30s. I qualified with a regional firm of accountants in the UK, where I gained extensive experience in accounting and tax services. My journey into the world of accounting started early, influenced by a deep interest in numbers and problem-solving.

Why I Became a Chartered Accountant

Growing up, I was always fascinated by how businesses operate and the pivotal role that finance plays in their success. This curiosity led me to pursue a degree in accounting and finance, where I discovered my knack for understanding complex financial systems and regulations. The structured and strategic nature of accounting appealed to my analytical mindset, and I decided to further my expertise by qualifying as a chartered accountant. The rigorous training and professional standards required for this qualification resonated with my commitment to excellence and continuous improvement.

Why I Want to Run My Own Business

After several years of working with a diverse range of clients at the regional firm, I realized I wanted more than just a conventional career path. The idea of running my own practice had always been in the back of my mind. Here's why:

1. **Empowering Female Entrepreneurs**: I have a strong desire to support female entrepreneurs, helping them navigate the financial complexities of their businesses. I believe in the power of women-led businesses and want to contribute to their success by providing tailored accounting and advisory services.

2. **Flexibility and Autonomy**: Running my own practice allows me the flexibility to work from anywhere and manage my time effectively. This autonomy enables me to create a work-life balance that suits my lifestyle and personal commitments.

3. **Innovation and Personal Touch**: I want to build a practice that leverages technology to provide efficient, real-time financial insights. At the same time, I aim to offer a personal touch that larger firms

often lack, fostering strong, trust-based relationships with my clients.

Purpose and Vision

Purpose: My purpose is to empower female entrepreneurs by providing them with the financial clarity and strategic insights needed to grow their businesses. I am committed to making accounting accessible and less intimidating, helping my clients feel confident in their financial decisions.

Vision: My vision is to create a virtual accountancy practice that becomes a trusted partner for female entrepreneurs across the UK. I envision a practice that stands out for its innovative use of technology, personalized service, and a deep understanding of the unique challenges faced by women in business.

I aim to build a community where my clients feel supported, informed, and inspired. By outsourcing certain functions like bookkeeping to experts, I can focus on providing high-level advisory services that drive real value for my clients.

Core Values:

- **Integrity**: Upholding the highest standards of honesty and transparency in all interactions.
- **Empowerment**: Equipping clients with the knowledge and tools to make informed financial decisions.
- **Innovation**: Continuously seeking better ways to serve clients using cutting-edge technology.
- **Client-Centricity**: Placing clients' needs at the forefront, ensuring personalized and responsive service.

Running my own business is more than just a career choice; it's a way to align my professional skills with my passion for supporting women in business. I'm excited about the journey ahead and the opportunity to make a meaningful impact on my clients' success.

David's email to Meera regarding her personal safety

To: Meera Desai (meeradesai@gmail.com)
From: David Henderson (david@hendersonaccounting.co.uk)
Subject: Personal safety

Hi Meera

Ensuring your personal safety when meeting prospective clients and introducers is important. Here are practical steps you can take to minimise risks, including considerations about learning self-defence:

Meeting Safety Measures

1. Meet in public places:
   - Always arrange to meet in well-populated, public locations such as coffee shops, business centres, or co-working spaces.

2. Inform someone:
   - Let a trusted friend or family member know the details of your meeting, including the location, time, and who you are meeting.

PRACTICE!

3. Share your location:

    ▫ Use a location-sharing app like Life360 or bSafe to share your real-time location with someone you trust during the meeting. bSafe allows you to share your location, send SOS signals, and even set up fake calls.

4. Virtual meetings:

    ▫ Where possible, suggest a virtual meeting instead of an in-person one. Tools like Zoom, Microsoft Teams, or Google Meet are excellent for this.

5. First impressions:

    ▫ Conduct initial meetings over video calls to get a sense of the person before deciding to meet in person.

6. Research:

    ▫ Do some research on the prospective client or introducer. Check their LinkedIn profile, company website, and any available online presence to verify their legitimacy.

7. Transportation:

    ▫ Arrange your own transportation to and from meetings. Avoid relying on the other party for a ride.

8. Arrival Time:

    ◦ Arrive early to scope out the location and ensure it feels safe. It also gives you the chance to select a suitable spot. Always have an exit strategy. Know the layout of the venue, including where the exits are located.

9. Emergency Contacts:

    ◦ Have a list of emergency contacts readily available on your phone. Know the local emergency numbers.

10. Trust Your Gut:

    ◦ If something feels wrong, don't hesitate to leave the situation. Your safety is more important than any meeting.

During the Meeting

1. Stay aware:

    ◦ Remain vigilant and aware of your surroundings. Trust your instincts and leave if something feels off.

2. Keep personal items close:

    ◦ Ensure your personal items, such as your phone and keys, are always easily accessible.

3. Positioning:
    - Choose a seat that allows you to see the entrance and exit. Avoid secluded areas or sitting with your back to the door.
4. Set boundaries:
    - Clearly establish professional boundaries from the outset. Be assertive if someone makes you uncomfortable.

Personal Presentation

1. Professional appearance:
    - Dress professionally and confidently. This can sometimes deter inappropriate behaviour.
2. Confidence:
    - Project confidence in your body language and communication. People who appear confident are less likely to be targeted.
3. Personal alarm:
    - Carry a personal alarm that can emit a loud noise to attract attention in an emergency.

After the Meeting

1. Check-In:
    - After the meeting, inform the person you previously notified that the meeting is over, and you are safe.

2. Follow-Up:

    ◌ Reflect on the meeting. If there were any red flags, consider whether this is someone you want to continue working with.

Learning self-defence

Learning self-defence can be an empowering and practical step towards ensuring your personal safety. Many gyms and community centres offer specific self-defence classes designed to teach practical techniques quickly. There are reputable online courses and tutorials available that can provide basic self-defence training.

While learning a martial art or self-defence can provide added security and confidence, the key to personal safety lies in preparation, awareness, and taking proactive measures. Combining these strategies will help ensure your safety when meeting prospective clients and introducers.

If you have any more specific concerns or need further advice, feel free to ask!

David

Meera's Customer Segments

Ambitious female entrepreneurs seeking growth:
- **Profile:** Women who are passionate about scaling their businesses and are looking for strategic financial guidance to achieve their goals.
- **Needs:** These entrepreneurs need financial clarity, strategic insights, and a trusted partner who understands the unique challenges they face as women in business. They value innovation, technology, and personalised service that helps them make confident financial decisions.
- **How I'll empower them:** By providing accessible, jargon-free accounting services, coupled with high-level strategic advice,

Female founders new to entrepreneurship:
- **Profile:** Women who are just starting their entrepreneurial journey and may find accounting and financial management intimidating or overwhelming.
- **Needs:** These clients seek a supportive and educational partner who can demystify accounting, offer financial literacy, and help them establish a solid financial foundation for their businesses.

- **How I'll empower them**: Through clear, straightforward financial advice and educational resources, I'll make accounting accessible and less intimidating

Established female-owned businesses:

- **Profile**: Female entrepreneurs who are managing established businesses but are navigating significant transitions, such as expansion, restructuring, or entering new markets.
- **Needs**: These clients need strategic advisory services, advanced financial planning, and innovative technology solutions to manage change effectively while maintaining financial stability.
- **How I'll empower them**: By offering personalised, high-level advisory services and leveraging cutting-edge financial technology, I'll help these women navigate transitions smoothly, capitalise on growth opportunities, and sustain long-term success.

Socially conscious female-led enterprises:

- **Profile**: Women leading purpose-driven businesses, such as social enterprises or nonprofits, who require financial management that aligns with their mission and values.
- **Needs**: These clients need financial clarity and strategic advice that support both their financial sustainability and their social impact goals.
- **How I'll empower them**: By offering financial insights that align with their mission.

10 Step Discovery Call process

Remaining flexible during your discovery calls is crucial to their success but it is still worth using a call outline. Keep it bullet pointed so it doesn't sound as if you are reading from a script and remember to record the call, if possible, or at the very least take notes. When you listen back to a recorded call, you'll hear things you didn't hear on the original call.

Step1: Establish rapport and take control
- Say hello and introduce yourself
- Confirm the reason for the call
- Then, let's crack on with the call, shall we? ...
  - How this call will go best is I'll start by asking you some questions about your business and your goals...
  - Then, if it sounds like I can help you, I'll explain what I have to offer and how everything works.
  - Then, at the end, you can decide as to whether you want to be part of it or not. Does that sound like a plan?

- Wait for them to say, "Yes that's OK," before moving forward.

Step 2: Understand their problem or pain

- You need to understand what's going on in their business and why they're looking for help? If you get a good answer, that's great, replay it back to them to make sure you've understood and move on.
- On some calls you'll need dig a little deeper, in which case the following questions can work quite well:
    - Why do you think you've got this problem?
    - What have you tried to do to fix this?
    - Tell me more…

Step 3: Understand their business

- Get a good understanding of their business
    - Talk me through exactly what you sell.
    - Who is your ideal customer?
    - Why do your customers choose you over your competitors?
    - So how do you currently get customers? What's working well?
- Be GENUINELY interested in their business
- Make it sound like a conversation not an interrogation.

Step 4: Agitate their pain (you'll need to customise this section to your own business)

- Ask questions that will make them realise there is a cost to carrying on as they are

- Do you know how much it's costing you having to do your own books?
- Do you have a process in place for getting new customers?
- Are you comfortable relying on this way of working to run your business?
- Get personal. (Don't skip this part of the process)
  - How much money are <u>you</u> taking per month from the business right now?
  - What do you pay yourself?
  - How do you feel about that? Is it enough?
- Get a specific amount per month that they're drawing from the business.
- This is really important to help you with the close at the end, AND to get them associating you - and relating your service - to their income.

Step 5: Get them to tell you what they want

- If you could wave a magic wand, where do you want the business to be in 12 months' time? *You MUST get an answer to this question.*
- Get a specific figure around turnover or profit or their drawings before you move forward.
- Find out why they want that?
  - What's your motivation? Why does it matter to you?
  - How would things be different for you in the business when you get to that?
  - How will getting to that impact on other areas of your life and family?

- Help them to visualise a situation better than where they are now.
- Some people will aim too low. They won't be able to visualise a situation that is <u>markedly</u> different from where they are now.
- Help them to aim higher and widen what's possible for them.

Step 6: Transition

- What's stopping you from achieving that on your own?
- Get one of these statements from them or, ideally, more than one!
    - They are unable to do it on their own.
        - They <u>don't know how</u> to do it on their own.
        - They want to delegate it so they have more time.
        - They want better information.
        - They want to follow a proven system and/or have help and support.

Step 7: Get commitment

- I can see that you want to fix it, but how committed are you to making it happen?
- Are you sure you don't want to just stay where you are?
- There's always a powerful reason behind why somebody wants to go through change. You just need to find it.

PRACTICE!

Step 8: Tell them how you can help (you'll need to customise this section to your own business)
- I can definitely help you with that. Shall I explain to you what I do?
- Well, my area of expertise is helping businesses just like yours to [explain what you do in one sentence]
    - Get and keep their books up to date so they know their business numbers.
    - Crack what we call the rhythmic acquisition of customers.
- I work with small businesses just like yours and help them to drive the profitability that the business owner needs so that their drawings go up to the level they want by putting in place-
    - the right cloud accounting system so that they know what decisions to take.
    - the right marketing and sales processes so they consistently and predictably get and keep the right level of customers.
- That's what we do and that's what we're really good at, so it looks like we're a perfect fit
- DON'T go into detail about how it all works. Now shut up.
- You want to get really comfortable and good at saying this. It will need practise.
- You want your prospect to think, "Yes, that's what I need" and "That's exactly where I am right now..." and "That's exactly what I want to achieve..."

Step 9: Answer their questions and objections

- Keep quiet; your prospect must be the one to talk next. If you've done everything properly so far, they'll likely ask something about how it works
- Answer their questions honestly, and concisely but talk about things at a high level
- Do NOT get sucked into the detail of the processes or the features or anything like that.
- Keep everything focused on the OUTCOME for them – and where possible use THEIR language to describe those outcomes.
- Keep answering their questions until they have a clear understanding and are happy.
- As you answer their questions, be careful not to divert the conversation. Just answer their specific question and then shut up.
- Eventually, when your prospect has asked all the questions they have, they'll ask you about price...

Step 10: Explain the price of your service

- This part only comes when your prospect asks for it. Say something like:
- "My fee for setting up your cloud accounting and doing your bookkeeping for a business of your size is normally £1,000 per month, and there is a setup fee of £1,000. But I found that those who make decisions quickly always turn out to be the best clients and we do amazing work together. So, for that reason, if you make a decision on the call with me today, I'll waive that £1,000 setup fee and it's just £1,000 per month."

PRACTICE!

- Then shut up. **Your silence here is the most crucial part of your entire call.** Remain silent until your prospect speaks. What you're waiting for here is words that mean they want to move forward with this. Things like:
    - What's the next step?
    - OK, well, what's next?
    - OK, how do we get started?
    - OK, let's do it!"
- You mustn't accept anything here that does not mean either yes or no.

Handling objections

1. How much time do I have to decide?

    How much time do you need to decide? Is there something you need to think about that we can discuss right now?" [Flesh that out and talk about it.]

2. I need time to find the money.

    When will you be looking over your finances? See 4. below

3. I just don't make decisions on the spot.

    When will you be sitting down to think about it and decide? See 4. below

4. I need to talk with my partner or spouse...

    When specifically, will you be talking with your partner or spouse? NB: *offer to get on the phone with the spouse or partner and discuss it too. It can work really well when you do.*

    Perfect. So, you'll have spoken with your spouse or partner (or looked over your finances) by tomorrow evening... get enrolled by 6:00pm tomorrow and I'll hold those savings for you until then. *[If they can decide in 24 (or 48) hours, just give them a specific time and day that they need to enrol by to get your incentive price.]*

5. I haven't got the money.

Okay... PAUSE!! I understand that finances can sometimes be a challenge, and we always do our best to work with people so let me ask you this, is this something that you really want to do? Because if it's not a good fit for you that's OK... *(They'll usually respond with "Oh no, I really wanted to do it...").* So how can we make this happen for you?

6. Objection: I can't afford it.

Tell me more about that... *(Let them talk to you about this...)* OK, so you just shared with me on this call exactly what you need to do move forward. So how are you going to afford to continue without doing that? So how can we make this a reality for you?

7. Objection: Once I make some money then I want to work with you.

Okay, so tell me how that would work? *Let them talk...* Okay, let's see if I've got this right. What you're saying is that you're going to continue to do what you've told me is building your business really slowly and isn't even paying your bills. And you're going to continue to do what's not working long enough until someday you've built up some surplus cash that you can invest in what will work. Is that an accurate assessment of what you just said...*Done properly they'll realise how silly they sound...* So how can I make this work for you...?

8. Objection: I need some time to think it over.

Absolutely, I get that. I want to make sure this is a great fit for you. Can I just ask though what haven't we discussed that you still need to think about? *Wait for response.* It's just that's why I take the time to do these calls properly. I'm here right now to help you make the right decision. All I want is for you to do what's right for you. While you've still got me on the phone what questions or concerns do you have that I haven't answered?

[If they can decide in 24 (or 48) hours, just give them a specific time and day that they need to enrol by to get your incentive price.]

9. Objection: It's not a good time.

So, when would be a good time for you to start putting in place the things that you've said are most important to you?

10. Objection: I've been in other programmes like this, and I still haven't got the results I wanted.

It sounds like there's somebody you don't trust here and it's either me or you. Which do you think it is, because we ought to discuss it… What specific outcomes would you need to see to make this totally worth the investment of your time and resources? What would make it a complete no brainer for you?

Do you have a guarantee?

Absolutely. I guarantee that if you keep doing what you're doing, you won't [solve the problem] and you'll continue to get the same sorts of results.

Now, with that said, I also guarantee that my system works. But if you're looking for an 'out' before you begin then I'm probably not a good fit for you.

It's all good either way but if you commit to this it should be with the attitude that this is going to work for you fully and completely, or you decide that it's not right for you at this time and it's not a good fit that's totally okay… In my experience, people who are looking for a reason for something not to work usually find it.

The killer question

If your prospect is really on the fence then use this killer question:

'*The real decision you're making isn't about working with me or someone else. That's irrelevant. The real decision is whether you're ready to take your business where you want it to be. Until you're ready to change, nothing else matters.*'"

The reason this is a killer question is it makes their decision about getting what they want from their business and in life - not about working with you. They're not deciding to work with you or buy your service. They're making a decision on whether or not they want to stay stuck where they are or move forward and gain the things in life that they really want.

David's Client Data Questionnaire

Business name: Date:

Please complete the questions below as far as you are able. Your information will be kept strictly confidential.

	Owner 1	Owner 2 (if applicable)
Name		
Business name		
Registered office address Tel no		
Trading address Tel no		
Home address Tel no		

PERSONAL DETAILS		
Mobile telephone number		
email address		
Date of birth		
Nationality		
No. of years resident in UK		
National insurance number		
Unique tax reference (UTR)		
Self-assessment user id (if known)		
Self-assessment online password (if known)		
Passport number		
BUSINESS DETAILS		
Date of incorporation or start of business		
Registered number (company only)		
Co. House authentication code (company)		
Accounting reference date/year end		
Annual return due date (company only)		

PRACTICE!

Is the business a member of any trade association?		
Corporation tax reference number		
VAT number (if registered)		
Date of VAT registration (please attach your VAT certificate)		
VAT return quarters		
VAT online user id (if known)		
VAT online password		
PAYE reference number (if applicable)		
No. of directors		
No. of employees		
Name and address of previous Accountant Tel no		

Name and address of Solicitor Tel no		
Name and address of Bank		
Do you have an up to date will? If so, where is a copy kept?		

If there are any changes to the information provided above, please advise us as soon as possible.

Signed ....
Date ....

Checklist for a digital accountancy practice

1. Legal and Regulatory Compliance
   - Business Registration:
     - Register your business name with the relevant authorities.
     - Choose a suitable business structure (sole trader, partnership, limited company).
   - Licensing and Permits:
     - Obtain necessary licenses and permits for running an accountancy practice.
     - Ensure compliance with the Institute of Chartered Accountants' regulations.
   - Professional Indemnity Insurance:
     - Secure professional indemnity insurance to protect against claims of professional negligence.
   - Outsourcing Contracts:
     - Draft clear contracts for freelancers, outlining responsibilities, confidentiality, and data security requirements.
     - Ensure compliance with GDPR and other relevant data protection regulations when sharing client information with freelancers.

- Conduct thorough background checks and verify references for freelancers to ensure reliability and competence.

2. Financial and Tax Considerations
- Banking:
  - Open a dedicated business bank account.
- Funding:
  - Determine initial capital requirements and explore funding options if necessary.
- Tax Registration:
  - Register for VAT if applicable.
  - Set up PAYE if you plan to hire employees.
- Accounting Software:
  - Choose and subscribe to a cloud-based accounting software like Xero.
  - Subscribe to Xero and choose a plan that suits your business needs.
  - Complete Xero certification to ensure you can fully leverage the software's capabilities.
  - Set up Xero with your business details and customise the chart of accounts.
- Freelancer Payments:
  - Set up a system for tracking and managing payments to freelancers.
  - Consider using Xero's built-in features or integrating with payment platforms like PayPal or TransferWise for smooth transactions.

3. Technology and Infrastructure
- Hardware:

- Invest in a reliable computer and necessary peripherals (printer, scanner).
- Software:
  - Install professional accounting software.
  - Set up office suite software (Microsoft Office or Google Workspace).
  - Ensure Xero is integrated with your bank accounts for seamless transaction tracking.
  - Set up Xero add-ons and integrations that might be beneficial, such as Hubdoc for document management or Gusto for payroll processing.
  - Implement secure login procedures for Xero, such as two-factor authentication.
- Stay Updated with Xero:
  - Regularly participate in Xero webinars and training sessions to keep up with new features and best practices.
  - Join the Xero community forums and groups for peer support and networking.
- Explore the Xero App Marketplace:
  - Identify and integrate apps that enhance your practice, such as Receipt Bank for expense management, Futrli for forecasting, and Chaser for automated credit control.
- Internet:
  - Ensure high-speed internet connectivity.
- Data Security:
  - Implement robust cybersecurity measures.
  - Use secure cloud storage solutions for client data.
  - Collaboration Tools:

- Use project management and communication tools (e.g., Trello, Slack) to coordinate with freelancers.
- Data Access:
  - Provide secure access to Xero for freelancers handling payroll and bookkeeping, with appropriate permissions set to limit their access to necessary functions only.

4. Office Setup
   - Workspace:
     - Designate a dedicated workspace in your home.
     - Ensure ergonomic furniture for comfort and productivity.
   - Communication Tools:
     - Set up a professional email address.
     - Use a business phone number and consider VoIP solutions.
     - Establish video conferencing capabilities (Zoom, Microsoft Teams).
     - Use Xero's in-built communication tools to manage client interactions related to financial matters.
   - Communication Protocols:
     - Establish regular check-in meetings with freelancers to ensure alignment and address any issues promptly.
     - Set up a communication schedule and preferred methods (e.g., email, video calls) for ongoing collaboration.

5. Marketing and Client Acquisition
   - Branding:
     - Create a professional logo and brand identity.
     - Develop a business website showcasing your services and expertise.
   - Networking:
     - Join local business networks and online forums.
     - Attend industry events and webinars.
   - Marketing Strategy:
     - Utilise social media platforms to reach potential clients.
     - Consider content marketing (blogging, newsletters).
     - Implement SEO strategies for your website.

6. Client Management
   - Client Onboarding:
     - Develop a client onboarding process.
     - Create standard contracts and engagement letters.
     - Create a standard onboarding process in Xero, including setting up new clients and providing them with necessary access.
   - CRM System:
     - Explore Xero integrations with CRM tools to streamline client management and communication.
     - Implement a customer relationship management system.
   - Communication:
     - Use Xero's reporting features to provide clients with regular financial updates.

- ○ Set up regular communication protocols (emails, meetings).
- ○ Establish a feedback mechanism for continuous improvement.
- Client Data Handling:
  - ○ Create a protocol for how client data is shared with and accessed by freelancers, ensuring it meets security standards.
- Quality Control:
  - ○ Implement a review process to check the work done by freelancers before it's shared with clients.
  - ○ Establish clear reporting standards for freelancers, including frequency, format, and key metrics to be tracked.
  - ○ Implement a feedback mechanism to provide freelancers with constructive feedback and ensure continuous improvement.

7. Professional Development
   - Continuous Learning:
     - ○ Stay updated with the latest accounting standards and regulations.
     - ○ Attend professional development courses and seminars.
   - Certifications:
     - ○ Pursue relevant certifications to enhance your credentials.

8. Operational Processes
   - Workflow Management:

- Develop and document standard operating procedures.
- Use project management tools to track tasks and deadlines.
- Use Xero Practice Manager (if applicable) to manage workflow, track jobs, and allocate tasks.
* Billing and Invoicing:
  - Set up an efficient billing and invoicing system.
  - Set up Xero invoicing templates customised with your branding.
  - Automate recurring invoices and reminders for outstanding payments in Xero.
* Time Management:
  - Implement time-tracking tools to monitor productivity.
* Workflow Management:
  - Use tools like Xero Practice Manager or Asana to assign tasks and track the progress of outsourced work.
* Billing and Invoicing:
  - Ensure freelancers submit timesheets or reports on work completed to facilitate accurate billing and invoicing.

9. Support Services
   * Have access to legal advice for contract and compliance issues.
   * IT Support:
     - Ensure technical support for software and hardware issues.
     - Ensure freelancers have access to technical support for any issues related to software or access.

- Admin Assistance:
    - Consider virtual assistants for administrative tasks if needed.
- Freelancer Resources:
    - Provide freelancers with access to necessary resources and training to ensure they are up to date with Xero and your firm's procedures.

Onboarding checklist

Client name ....

This checklist is designed to guide you through the steps involved in giving a new client an awesome onboarding experience once they have been through your sales process and are ready to sign with your practice. Although every client is different there are some matters you'll want to cover with every client. Modify this checklist according to the needs of each new client.

Compliance	/	Date
Complete and document risk assessment.		
Carry out AML checks and obtain client photo identification and proof of address.		
Draft and send engagement letter including agreed fee and payment terms.		
Obtain signed engagement letter.		
Set up recurring billing of monthly fee in Xero.		

Create direct debit using GoCardless or other payment confirmation.		
Data gathering		
Send Client Data Questionnaire and monitor for return of completed form.		
Review completed Client Data Questionnaire for omitted items and follow-up.		
Send professional courtesy letter to previous accountant, if applicable.		
Obtain copies of Companies House filed documents		
Add documents to Practice Assurance file		
Welcome pack and introductory zoom call		
Draft welcome letter		
Create welcome pack documents to include contact information, FAQs etc.		
Send copies of books you've written with welcome pack		
Book introductory zoom call and send agenda		
Introduce bookkeeper and payroll specialist, if applicable		
Agree dates of monthly zoom calls, add to calendar and send client invitations		

Explain your 'way of working' and client responsibilities		
Set expectations and parameters for working together		
Give client Calendly link to book calls		
Answer questions from client and ask for feedback on onboarding process		
Set-up		
Request activation codes for tax from HMRC.		
Input tax activation codes in HMRC Agent portal.		
Create Xero file or obtain access and billing from previous accountant.		
Check that Xero opening balances agree to filed statutory accounts.		
Link VAT module in Xero to Agent Services Account, if applicable.		
Check VAT filing dates and add client to VAT control schedule		
Update Accounts control schedule with accounts and corporation tax filing dates.		
Check that corporation tax and VAT returns and payments are up to date		
Add the client to Inform Direct		

Add the owners/directors of the client to email list on Aweber after consent given.		
Follow client on relevant social media		
Change the registered office at Companies house, if applicable.		
Operations		
Add the details of each area of work and deadlines to control schedules		
Document our workflow for each area of work (accounts, tax etc.)		
Record completion and review of workflow tasks on checklists		
Monitor bookkeeping progress in Xero		
Prepare and issue monthly management report		
Team (including employees and freelancers), if applicable		
Introduce team members who will be working with the client		
Provide team member contact details (email and telephone)		
Assign responsibilities to team members		

Acknowledgements

Business Model Canvas (Page 24)

The Business Model Canvas is © Strategyzer.com and licensed under the Creative Commons Attribution-ShareAlike 3.0 Unported License (CC BY-SA 3.0). Used and adapted with permission. For details see www.strategyzer.com.

Marcus Sheridan – Knowledge Centre (Page 41)

In They Ask, You Answer, Marcus Sheridan introduced the idea of the Knowledge Centre as a prospect education tool. They Ask, You Answer Wiley; 2nd Edition, Revised and Updated (2019). Used for educational and illustrative purposes only.

Harvard Business Review – Generative AI Article (Page 72)

A recent article in Harvard Business Review outlined ways to train the mind for broader outcomes with generative AI. How Generative AI Can Augment Human Creativity by Tojin T. Eapen, Daniel J. Finkenstadt, Josh Folk and Lokesh Venkataswamy published in Harvard Business Review (July-August 2023) © 2023 Harvard Business Publishing. Insights referenced from Harvard Business Review articles on generative AI are used under fair dealing for commentary and educational purposes. No affiliation or endorsement is implied.

Boston Consulting Group – "Strategise Your Life" Framework (Page 94)

Adapted from Use Strategic Thinking to Create the Life You Want by Rainer Strack, Susanne Dyrchs, and Allison Bailey, published in Harvard Business Review (December 5, 2023, updated February 21, 2024). © 2024 Harvard Business Publishing. Used for illustrative and educational purposes only. All rights remain with the original authors. No affiliation or endorsement by BCG is implied.

Martin Seligman – PERMA Model (Pages 96–97)

The PERMA model, developed by Martin Seligman, outlines five pillars of wellbeing and is referenced from his book Flourish - A New Understanding of Happiness and Wellbeing: The practical guide to using positive psychology to make you happier and healthier (2011). Used for educational and illustrative purposes only.

Daniel Kahneman and Angus Deaton – Defining a Great Life (Page 96)

Reference to High income improves evaluation of life but not emotional well-being by Daniel Kahneman and Angus Deaton, published in Proceedings of the National Academy of Sciences (2010). Used under fair dealing for commentary. No affiliation or endorsement is implied.

Harvard Business Review / Clayton Christensen – 'How Will You Measure Your Life?' (Page 96)

A short quote and concept are adapted from Clayton M. Christensen's article "How Will You Measure Your Life?" published in Harvard Business Review (July–August 2010). © 2010 Harvard Business Publishing. Used under fair dealing for the purpose of commentary. No affiliation or endorsement is implied.

All third-party material is acknowledged with gratitude. Every effort has been made to ensure proper attribution. If any source has been unintentionally omitted or misrepresented, please contact the publisher so corrections can be made in future editions.

About the Author

For over five decades, Noel Guilford has dedicated his career to helping businesses and individuals thrive. He started his journey with a small two-partner accountancy firm, where a brief internship sparked a lifelong passion for numbers. After earning an accountancy degree, he qualified as a chartered accountant at Arthur Andersen & Co., taking on both auditing roles and the training of new graduates.

A turning point came when a respected firm, Spicer & Pegler, recruited him to launch a new office in Chester. He found premises, assembled a team, created a marketing plan, and grew the branch into the fastest-expanding office, swelling to a staff of over a dozen in three years. Later, he became a partner at one of the world's largest accountancy practices, Deloitte, but realised his most valuable lessons came from his time at Spicer & Pegler and eventually setting up his own firms.

Today, he runs Guilford Accounting, focusing on two key areas: providing compliance and advisory services to entrepreneurial business owners, and guiding fellow accountants who want to start their own practices. His approach is holistic, offering not just financial expertise but also mentoring on business strategy, marketing, and personal development.

He is a #1 best-selling author of How to Build a Successful Business (2018) and Business Maths Made Simple (2022).

Outside work, he stays motivated by reading, and his passion for sport—especially football, tennis, and cricket—provides a welcome balance to his professional life. Above all, he remains driven by the success of his clients, offering attentive, personalised support to each one, and continually embracing innovation to stay at the cutting edge of accountancy and business advisory.

You can contact him at noel@guilfordaccounting.co.uk and connect with him on LinkedIn at https://www.linkedin.com/in/noelguilford/.

I hope you found Practice! helpful in understanding the steps to take to start your own Accountancy practice. Writing this book has been a rewarding journey, and I sincerely appreciate you taking the time to read it.

*If you enjoyed the book or found it useful, I would truly appreciate it if you could take a moment to leave an **honest review** on Amazon. Your feedback helps other readers decide whether this book is right for them.*

Work with me

If you like what you've read in this book and want to spend some more time with me then here's what you can do next to get my support to help you grow your own successful digital accountancy practice that gives you more money, financial and time freedom.

Complete my practice health assessment checklist

Assess the health of your practice – or find out what best practice looks like for a digital accountancy practice – by completing my practice health assessment checklist. Find your gaps and prepare a practice improvement action plan: https://bit.ly/practice-health-check.

Work with me

If you are just starting out or want to grow your practice join my community of sole practitioners for one-to-one support You get the training, tools and support to create your ideal firm covering everything from compliance, marketing, getting clients, onboarding and operations. In fact, everything I cover in the book.

Every month you'll have a training session with me delivered virtually. You also get access to all the resources I've created and use in my own firm (checklists, templates, marketing materials etc.) that you can deploy to implement your training. Book a call with me at https://calendly.com/noelguilford/practice

Elite support to scale your practice

My elite support is for practice owners who've been in practice for at least 2-3 years and now want to expand their practice by taking on team members, accelerate their growth and get results faster. You get the training, tools and support to scale your firm covering everything from compliance, marketing, getting clients, onboarding, developing systems, recruiting and operations, and access to all the resources I've created and use in my own firm. Every month you'll have a training session with me delivered virtually. Book a call with me at https://calendly.com/noelguilford/practice

Book me to speak

If you're an event organiser or podcast host and would like me to speak at an event or on your podcast, email me at noel@guilfordaccounting.co.uk.